# Reflections *From*
## *The* Home Team...
## Nearing Home!

# Reflections *From* *The* Home Team... Nearing Home!

*As we all get closer to "Nearing Home" on our personal life journey's, our awards, trophies, diplomas, and job titles will fade. But striving to be first in love, showing up for others, and making our lives about something far bigger than ourselves will be remembered not only after our death, but will positively change the world while we are alive. Let's all strive to be first in that race!*

## David Welter

XULON ELITE

Xulon Press Elite
555 Winderley Pl, Suite 225
Maitland, FL 32751
407.339.4217
www.xulonpress.com

Paperback ISBN-13: 979-8-86850-510-2
Ebook ISBN-13: 979-8-86850-511-9

# *Dedication*

"Be joyful in hope, patient in affliction, faithful in prayer." Romans 12:12

P aul provided us these instructions for dealing with life's difficulties.

This book was written in loving memory of my parents, Bob and Rita, who taught me the importance of hard work and perseverance as well as how caring for and loving others is part of the purpose God has given each of us in this life. I have tried to pass those values to my three adult children, John, Rob and Sarah, their spouses as well as my precious grandchildren, Grace, Lucy, Hazel, and Finnegan.

A special thank you also to my "Home Team", who have faithfully stood by me on my life's journey. Your outpouring of love has provided me with the strength, encouragement, and support needed to move forward, one step at a time as I continue to work at being joyful in hope, patient in affliction, and faithful in prayer.

# Table of Contents

# *About the Author*

D avid Welter retired from the Cedar Falls Community School District in Cedar Falls, Iowa, after serving a for-ty-year career in education. Thirty-seven of those forty years were spent in Cedar Falls. During that time, Welter taught social studies and has been involved with baseball at the high school, college, and professional levels while also serving as a junior high principal for sixteen years in Cedar Falls.

Welter was diagnosed with cancer on his 55th birthday in February of 2009. He has written his stories, *Reflections from the Home Team... Go the Distance, Reflections from the Home Team... STAYING POSITIVE When Life Throws You a Curve! Reflections from the Home Team... Reframing the Curveballs Life Pitches Our Way!*, and *Reflections from the Home Team... NEARING HOME!* in an effort to share the hardships, emotions, support and hope he has encountered on his journey with cancer since being diagnosed. He often uses baseball metaphors and analogies to help communicate his thoughts as he is most comfortable sharing those thoughts by connecting them to that important part of his life.

Coaching and educating young people have formed the core of Welter's life over the years. His passion and love for his students, staff, and athletes are clearly demonstrated in his writing as he attempts to inspire a positive mindset for those struggling with cancer as well as other life challenges that may come their way.

Since retiring, Welter continues to scout for the Atlanta Braves, has worked as an education consultant, farms, and enjoys precious time with his grandchildren. Welter has been inducted into the Iowa High School Baseball Coaches Hall of Fame, the Cornell College Athletics Hall of Fame as well as being named Iowa's Middle Level Principal of the Year.

# Foreword

*in inceptum finis est* =
### "the beginning foreshadows the end."

I met my friend, Dave Welter – a highly respected school administrator, teacher, coach, and scout for the Atlanta Braves – in early June of 2009 while he served on the Call Committee of a congregation in Iowa. Subsequently, I was privileged to serve as that congregation's Senior Pastor for almost thirteen years. I learned early on that our first meeting came mere months after his initial and surprising diagnosis of stage-three throat cancer just as he was set to celebrate his fifty-fifth birthday.

In my capacity as one of Dave's pastors, I have had a front row seat, or what baseball insiders might refer to as a "scout seat" behind his "home plate" where I have watched his cancer journey unfold – every pitch, every swing! Dave's strength and humility, grace and wisdom, sensitivity and insight, faith and hope have characterized his journey from beginning to end.

*in inceptum finis est* =
### "the beginning foreshadows the end."

Right away, Dave began to process his thoughts and emotions by putting pen to paper; by journaling and detailing his cancer battle through daily reflections and devotions, powerful anecdotes, analogies, and encouraging stories that were a natural expression and extension of the man so many have trusted as a teacher, coach, and mentor through the years. By 2017 Dave had compiled and published his first book, entitled, *Reflections from the Home Team: Go the Distance*.

Indeed, over these years he has "Gone the Distance", allowing his own trials, tragedies, and triumphs to speak into the lives of numerous readers through a series of *Reflections from the Home Team*, of which this book is the fourth install-ment. Along the way, each subsequent book has served as a source of inspiration and encouragement for others whose own life circumstances have encountered "curve balls" and "extra innings" requiring personal resilience, the guidance of coaches, and the encouragement of each one's "Home Team."

### *in inceptum finis est =*
### "the beginning foreshadows the end."

In *Reflections from the Home Team: NEARING HOME!* Dave asks: "How will I be remembered after I'm gone?" This inquiry leads to other questions, like: "Am I investing my life in the things that matter most? Am I spending the limited time I have on this earth in fulfillment of my life's purpose? Am I nurturing deep, loving relationships with people, especially those who are close to me? Am I living each day in a way that reflects the presence and grace of Christ?"

While I don't presume to know your circumstances, chal-lenges, or aspirations, or whether you find yourself in your first or final inning, I pray Dave's words and insights may guide and strengthen you. For each day of this life that passes finds all of us "Nearing Home!" And if the Latin saying is indeed true that, "the begin-ning foreshadows the end," then may this "Foreword" urge you forward into the pages, "innings," and encourage-ment which follows!

Pastor Brian King
Chisago Lake Lutheran Church
Center City, Minnesota

# Introduction

T hank you for your interest in *Reflections from the Home Team... NEARING HOME!* My name is David Welter, and I am a retired teacher, coach and Principal in Cedar Falls, Iowa. I have been on a "cancer journey" since being diagnosed on my 55th birthday back in 2009. It's been a journey with many ups and downs... Since that time, I have focused on renewing my mind, almost daily, when seeking healing, whether that be physical, emotional, or spiritual healing.

I carry with me in my heart a special verse from Proverbs each day to remind me of the importance of renewing my mind with positive thoughts each and every day as I face the challenges that accompany a cancer journey...

> "A happy heart is good medicine, and a cheerful mind works healing, but a broken spirit dries up the bones." Proverbs 17:22

I have experienced both sides of this in my heart since I began my cancer journey back in 2009. I've also seen both sides in many of the people I've been blessed to come across during that time. For me, a happy heart and cheerful mind is something I have to work at when the pains and struggles that accompany this journey challenge me.

I have discovered that our hearts and minds are intricately connected. It's impossible to have a happy heart when your mind is full of negative thoughts. Left to itself, our minds can become the "devil's workshop"– pulling us away from the joy and happiness we can experience, even in our difficult times. That is when we need to seek help in replacing those negative thoughts with the help of family, friends, and yes, God with the promise of His unfailing love for each of us.

I think back to many of the "strangers" I sat with at the University of Iowa Hospital in Iowa City and at Mayo Clinic in Rochester during treatments. Many of us faced similar challenges and I so enjoyed many of the "unscripted" conversations I had with those complete strangers. I was often unsure of how to start many of those conversations, but in each case, I set aside my fear and began an unscripted conversation. In these unexpected moments, God provided the opportunity to discuss with each how a positive attitude, and a joyful heart could help us overcome the difficult situations we were facing. We often visited about overcoming challenges and the changes happening in our lives. These were people, perhaps like you, who were trying to bring about positive change in their lives given the "curveball" life had pitched them... Many, including myself, felt overwhelmed, unsure of what to do next, questioning themselves and their ability to keep moving forward.

Sometimes, those questions drive us into hiding rather than into a time of sharing. My cancer journey has led me to a deeper relationship with not only God, but with others whose life journeys have intersected with mine. By not fearing or hiding from the risk of sharing our stories with each other in those unexpected encounters, we're able to exchange that fear of rejection for the courage to share how together, we can offer each other the support and strength needed to overcome our life's many challenges; YES, even the challenges we may face on a cancer journey! Given those thoughts, I have written this book to share how stories of perseverance and a positive mindset can help us reframe those challenges for the better when facing the "curveballs" life may pitch our way.

Aside from my own family and my faith, three things have had a major impact on my life, those being Education, Coaching and Baseball. I want you to know I have been very blessed in my educational career knowing both the frustration as well as the satisfaction of working with young people. Sometimes we all need an inspirational boost to remember the love and passion that ultimately motivate us all. One of the best ways to remind each other of the value of what we do is through the telling of stories, inspiring stories, so please allow me the opportunity to share some of those stories that have impacted me as a husband, a father, a teacher, a coach and as a principal in the pages that follow.

*Reflections from the Home Team...NEARING HOME!* is intended to be a resource you can turn to each day for hope and encouragement as you take on the daily challenges that life may "pitch" your way. The book is a go-to resource for injecting a healthy dose of positivity into your daily life. Positivity has been proven to make a difference in overcoming negativity and adversity, and each reflection in the book examines positive perspectives and approaches to dealing with life challenges.

Each reflection includes an encouraging attitude, a spiritual insight, and a step to consider which are frequently blended with baseball analogies and metaphors. Life's challenges are not easy, just as baseball isn't always easy. The game provides many lessons about success and failure, and those lessons can often be applied in each of our life journeys. As life's challenges come your way, I encourage you to reach out to your personal "Home Team" (both human and divine) for the strength, love, support, and comfort needed to meet them.

Many of the thoughts I share in this book are not original thoughts, but rather reflect what I have read or discussed with others who may be experiencing similar challenges in their life journeys. These thoughts have helped me develop caring and loving relationships with family, friends, students, staff and even strangers. These precious connections, which I refer to as my "Home Team", have been so important on my personal journey.

This book can be used as a daily reflection to find a way forward, one step at a time, to help create some positive momentum whenever you may feel discouraged and need a boost. I'm hopeful you will find this book helpful as you open it to any page where you may find a message of encouragement that may help you get through whatever challenge you may be facing while providing not only inspiration for yourself, but for others as well. Be nourished by its positivity in the face of life's challenges.

As I'm getting older, my next birthday cake will require room for a bit more than 70 candles, so I'll most likely need a fire extinguisher to blow them all out! My hair is grayer, and my hourglass has much more sand on the bottom than on the top...

Given all that, I'm not only concerned about the present, but I'm also curious about the future. As each of us get closer to *"Nearing Home"* on our personal life journeys, our awards, trophies, diplomas, and job titles will fade. But striving to be first in love, showing up for others, and making our lives about something far bigger than ourselves will be remembered not only after our death, but will positively change the world while we are alive. Let's all strive to be first in that race!

# Reflection 1

# *Seeking Wisdom in our Lives...*

*July 17, 2022*

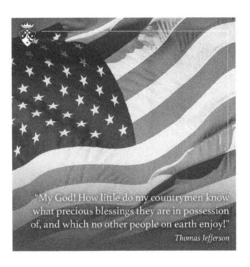

"My God! How little do my countrymen know what precious blessings they are in possession of, and which no other people on earth enjoy!"

*Thomas Jefferson*

*As we move forward on our life journeys, whatever direction that may take each of us, sharing a hospitable space with others as we share our beliefs and opinions, while focusing on God's word, Jesus's love and depending on the Holy Spirit's guidance, we can make a positive impact and truly make a difference in our world... Let the journey continue!*

You may recall that in my previous reflections, I have mused about the importance of seeking wisdom in our lives. Most importantly, seeking God's wisdom in our lives, because yes— God does know a thing or two, because He has seen a thing or two!

My quiet time this morning focused on hope... I couldn't help but think of the times in my life that I've felt discouragement when challenges have come my way. I often refer to them in my writing as I reflect on the faith and trust I place in God to give me the hope I need to carry on when those challenging times come my way. I've been leaning on Him a lot lately...

Sometimes it is hard to rediscover hope when bad things happen. But scripture confirms that God's goodness prevails through it all. He never forgets the needs of His people. Psalm 9:18 says,

> "But God will never forget the needy; the hope
> of the afflicted will never perish."

I am so thankful for that promise because even in the darkest times, hope will ultimately win.

When at times I feel myself giving in to discouragement, I think of Psalm 33:20...

> "We put our hope in the Lord. He is our help
> and our shield."

Today, tomorrow, and in the future to come, my hope will always remain in Him.

At this morning's service, Pastor Brian shared a message about unity, something that is sorely lacking in our country today. Pastor Brian used a verse from Luke 10:38-42 to emphasize the importance of hospitality when dealing with each other, no matter what our political, economic, social or for that matter any other leanings may be.

The story of Martha and Mary in this verse while entertaining Jesus speaks to the importance of providing a nurturing space as we entertain each other while sharing our thoughts, opinions, and beliefs even though they may differ. Sometimes, as I watch and listen to friends argue and debate things, I recall a quote Thomas Jefferson shared with James Madison in the early days of our Country when things may have seemed just as chaotic. Thomas Jefferson wrote this to James Monroe in a private message...

> "My God, how little do my countrymen know what precious blessings they are in possession of, and which no other people on earth enjoy!" [1]

Jefferson was right both then and now... We too often take for granted the things we enjoy as freedoms which have been fought and died for over nearly 250 years...

I would respectfully add the following to Pastor Brian's message this morning. The best place to look for calm in the midst of life's storms is the Bible, if not just for the guidance of Jesus through the apostles' writings, but also to see how countless Bible figures navigated their own turmoil.

King David was definitely one who let God know when he felt overwhelmed, but he did so knowing that whatever was difficult for him wouldn't be for God. Many people look to the book of Psalms to see the example of an overwhelmed Christian taking his concerns where they will be changed for the better – to God.

> "Peace, I leave with you, My peace I give to you; not as the world gives do I give you. Let not your heart be troubled, neither let it be afraid" (John 14:27).

When I feel as though the cares of this world are too much and that God doesn't care what happens to me (which I know is not the case, but at times doubt creeps into my thoughts), this verse demonstrates He wants everything I may be worried

3

about to be given to Him to be made better. No matter how minor or major my needs be, God wants to do great things with them.

There probably aren't many people in the world today who can say they aren't feeling overwhelmed in some area of their lives. There seems to be more upside-down in our world than right side up, and the Bible warns us of this as a reminder that our real home is not here, but elsewhere.

However, being overwhelmed just presents us with the opportunity to turn our attention back to God, back to His Word, and back to realizing that feeling overwhelmed is only temporary if we keep moving forward. We can be shocked by what is happening in this world, but we can also know that if we keep our eyes on God and believe He will use these times for good, we will see the blessings in disguise.

So, yes, it is okay to be overwhelmed as a Christian (we all experience that at times), for it gives us the chance to make the choice to keep following Jesus to see the fruits of that choice in helping ourselves and others be manifested in God's will. I resonate with Pastor Brian's closing this morning and my HOPE is that we can each provide a place and space for true hospitality as we share each other's thoughts and aspirations for this beautiful country we call our home...

> *"The purpose of hospitality is to provide an*
> *environment and space where relationships can*
> *be nurtured and can grow without distraction.*
> *May we come to know that true hospitality is*
> *achieved not only when we share our things, but*
> *each other."* [2]

As we move forward on our journeys, whatever direction that may take each of us, sharing a hospitable space with others as we share our beliefs and opinions, while focusing on God's word, Jesus's love and depending on the Holy Spirit's guidance, we can make a positive impact and truly make a difference in our world... Let the journey continue!

*An Encouraging Attitude:*
"The purpose of hospitality is to provide an environment and space where relationships can be nurtured and can grow without distraction. May we come to know that true hospitality is achieved not only when we share our things, but each other." Pastor Brian King, Nazareth Lutheran Church

*A Spiritual Insight:*
*"We put our hope in the Lord. He is our help and our shield."* Psalm 33:20

*A Step to Consider:*
As we move forward on our life journeys, whatever direction that may take each of us, sharing a hospitable space with others as we share our beliefs and opinions, while focusing on God's word, Jesus's love and depending on the Holy Spirit's guidance, we can make a positive impact and truly make a difference in our world... Let the journey continue!

# Reflection 2

# *Give Each Day a Chance*

*August 12, 2022*

*"Do not despise these small beginnings, for the
Lord rejoices to see the work begin."*
*(Zech. 4:10).*

A s we prepare to close out a difficult year in 2022, I have
come to realize more than ever all the small things that
have become bigger for me. From eating in a restaurant to
seeing a movie, to physically being able to hug or shake hands
with a friend, I no longer discount the small aspects of life that
were once so accessible. The past two and a half years have
helped me recognize those small things and the large impact
they can have in my life.

I can take note of the small things. I can rejoice and be
grateful for food to eat, for a warm, comfortable place to rest

my feet and my head at night, or simply for the breath in my lungs. I can also realize that these small little things I often did not even notice are in fact blessings!

I was reading some of the materials I had saved from the year I was diagnosed with cancer back in 2009. I vividly recall the loss of one of my favorite baseball personalities, Sparky Anderson back in 2010 shortly after completing my treatments. The baseball world lost one of its most prized possessions the day he passed. Sparky Anderson was the prototypical manager for me. He was a no nonsense, hard-nosed motivator who was beloved by fans and his players.

While he was one of the winningest managers of all-time, there were also plenty of losses. That's just how baseball works; even the absolute best teams lose at least 50 games a year in a 162-game schedule, and for much of his career, Sparky did not handle the losses well. They ate him up inside, gnawed at him and caused him to lose sleep (kind of like the past two and a half years have been for us).

Finally, in 1989 with his Detroit Tigers team struggling, Sparky finally broke. Mental and physical exhaustion forced him to spend time away from his team in May of that year. During that period, he realized that he had to find a way to move on after losses if he wanted to continue managing. He needed something to HOPE for! When he returned to his team, he promised his wife that he would follow the advice she offered him in the quote below:

> *"All she asked was for me to give each day a chance. If a bad day comes along, just battle the day. A bad day lasts only 24 hours. If you can get through that bad one, a good day might follow. Take each day one at a time. Then leave it for what it is." -Sparky Anderson* [3]

I took that advice to heart when I read it, as I was struggling with the mental and physical exhaustion that accompanied my cancer treatments, especially as I spent time away from my family, my students, and staff. It was a good lesson that when we base our happiness on the outcome (which we almost always can't control) rather than the process (which we can control) we leave ourselves vulnerable to problems. Life does not need to be completely perfect for us to find something to smile about. When we appreciate the smaller things, we also can then rejoice even more in the big things when they come. Life deserves more celebration, for both the great and the small.

We all have individual talents and messages in our hearts that can be shared to help bring joy and happiness to others during challenging times. The world is just waiting for us to share them... Many might ask, "So what difference will my work make in encouraging others?" God's answer:

> *"Do not despise these small beginnings, for the Lord rejoices to see the work begin" (Zech. 4:10).*

My prayer for each of us...
Dear Heavenly Father,
Please help us to begin... Just BEGIN! What seems small to each of us might be huge to someone else!! Things may not always go our way, or we might not feel well, *but together, with YOU* we can find a way to battle through it with tomorrow being a fresh start offering us some HOPE taking one day at a time. In Your name we pray. Amen

I'm very much looking forward to a fresh start in 2023, how about you?

### *An Encouraging Attitude:*

"All she asked was for me to give each day a chance. If a bad day comes along, just battle the day. A bad day lasts only 24 hours. If you can get through that bad one, a good day might follow. Take each day one at a time. Then leave it for what it is." -Sparky Anderson

### *A Spiritual Insight:*

*"Do not despise these small beginnings, for the Lord rejoices to see the work begin" (Zech. 4:10).*

### *A Step to Consider:*

Please help us to begin... Just BEGIN! What seems small to each of us might be huge to someone else!! Things may not always go our way, or we might not feel well, *but together, with YOU* we can find a way to battle through it with tomorrow being a fresh start offering us some HOPE taking one day at a time.

# Reflection 3

## *Beautifully Broken…*

*August 22, 2022*

*If everybody loved like Jesus, there'd be a lot less broken ones…*
**Jerry Salley, The Broken Ones**

The past 10 months have been challenging ones for myself and for several family members and friends. We all go through hard seasons in life and recently I have had to walk with some very dear friends through dark valleys as they deal with the loss of loved ones and friends. Saying goodbye is difficult as we reach that stage in our lives when those good-byes unfortunately become more common. It's probably best to say "see you later" while rejoicing in the hope of our heavenly reunion someday.

I enjoy all music genres, but a good friend recently shared a song from blue grass singer, songwriter and producer Jerry Salley that truly touched my heart. It's titled *The Broken Ones...* and the lyrics filled my heart with warm memories of my small-town upbringing, growing up on a farm here in Cedar Falls. I absolutely fell in love with his lyrical storytelling. In the lyrics, he emphasizes just how much Jesus truly loves the Broken Ones.

The lyrics describe a little girl named Maggie who pulls a Raggedy Ann doll out of a neighbor's trash can. The doll is missing an arm and one button eye hangs on by a thread. She finds a place for this broken one with her other dolls. The chorus is very touching for me as it describes the heart of this young girl.

> *She loves the broken ones, the ones that need a little patching up.*
>
> *She sees the diamond in the rough and makes it shine like new.*
>
> *It really doesn't take that much, a willing heart and a tender touch.*
>
> *If everybody loved like she does, there'd be a lot less broken ones.*[4]

Years later Maggie is working at a shelter when a young drug addict stumbles in lost and hopeless. Maggie embraces her and invites this broken soul into that safe place. She helps the young woman find healing. The lyrics go on to describe how many viewed Maggie as a hero because of her heart for those who are broken. She goes on to defer the credit to someone else... If you call her and angel, she'll be quick to say to you that she's just doing what the One who died for her would do.

She was simply doing what Jesus does. He loved the broken ones. The song ends with this addition to the chorus. "If everybody loved like Jesus, there'd be a lot less broken ones…"

Amen. The message of the song is spot on and is a message I needed to hear. Jesus loves the broken ones. This journey we all face in life is not easy. Never will be. One of the big mistakes we often tend to make in sharing our faith is making it seem like all troubles are over when you embrace Christianity. Unfortunately, that is not in the contract. We will still have problems and heartaches and even tragedies. King David wrote these words while escaping down a broken road…

> *The LORD is close to the brokenhearted;*
> *He rescues those who are crushed in spirit.*
> *Psalm 34:18*

There are so many brokenhearted people who simply need a caring heart. I know my *"Home Team"* has so often been there for me through my difficult times when my heart has been heavy. We often tend to condemn those who may appear broken hearted, not really knowing the reason why they may be struggling through life's problems and heartaches. Christian author Warren Wiersbe beautifully describes why we should not be quick to condemn those who appear to be struggling…

> *"I am not as critical as I used to be, not because*
> *my standards are lower, but because my sight is*
> *clearer. What I thought were blemishes in others*
> *have turned out to be scars." Warren Wiersbe* [5]

In the Gospel of John, Jesus talked about the Holy Spirit coming to be our advocate and comforter on this earth. He left this amazing promise that I cling to more fervently every day. "I am leaving you with a gift—peace of mind and heart. And the peace I give is a gift the world cannot give. So don't be troubled or afraid" (John 14:27).

I am experiencing that peace even now as both I and those that I care about and love experience difficult seasons in our lives. I am not afraid because I know without a doubt that He loves the broken ones. That is my assurance today.

Here is a link to Jerry's song if interested in listening...

The Broken Ones by Jerry Salley:
https://www.youtube.com/watch?v=C6ov6N9l9XQ

May we all be kind and offer encouragement to those in our lives who may be experiencing brokenness on their life journey.

### *An Encouraging Attitude:*
May we all be kind and offer encouragement to those in our lives who may be experiencing brokenness on their life journey.

### *A Spiritual Insight:*
*The LORD is close to the brokenhearted; He rescues those who are crushed in spirit. Psalm 34:18*

### *A Step to Consider:*
There are so many brokenhearted people who simply need a caring heart. I know my *"Home Team"* has so often been there for me through my difficult times when my heart has been heavy. We often tend to condemn those who may appear broken hearted not really knowing the reason they may be struggling through life's problems and heartaches.

In the Gospel of John, Jesus talked about the Holy Spirit coming to be our advocate and comforter on this earth. He left this amazing promise that I cling to more fervently every day. "I am leaving you with a gift—peace of mind and heart. And the peace I give is a gift the world cannot give. So don't be troubled or afraid" (John 14:27).

14

# Reflection 4

# *Help Others, Even When They Can't Help Back!*

*September 29, 2022*

*We have a chance daily to make others feel welcomed and loved. We have an opportunity to remind them that they matter and that their life is a gift. It might, in fact, be the most important thing they learn this school year! Don't miss the chance to teach it to them today. Help others, even when you know they can't help you back...*

This past weekend brought back many memories as I participated in my Columbus High School Class of '72 reunion. It was a wonderful weekend sharing stories and memories with some lifelong friends that I had established back in my High School days. It also brought back some wonderful memories of the times I spent in the education field over the past years. My inspiration to become a teacher, coach and eventually a principal all started at Columbus High school and was triggered by a wonderful man who served as my Principal at Columbus, Fr. Walter Brunkan. Fr. Brunkan passed away recently at the age of 92 and will be remembered in the hearts of many for his kindness and servant attitude.

For many, the start of school ushers in a welcome shift from summer. It means reunion with friends, the return of routine and the familiar sights, sounds and smells of the school building. Yes, we may miss the freedom of summer, but it's certainly a joy to be surrounded by others in places we feel welcome, are encouraged to learn, and fit in with others. For many, this is a wonderful transition. For many. But not for all. One of my goals as a building principal was to make school a welcoming place for all; a place where students were encouraged to learn and fit in with others.

My life odometer, and I'm guessing yours, seems to keep adding mileage, imagine that... no matter how hard I try I cannot roll it back. Part of acquiring higher mileage is getting some hard-earned perspective on your life decisions. Some of my decisions were good. Some benign. Some not so good. That is life. The encouragement I have discovered is that even the poor decisions we may make can be redeemed by the grace of God.

D.L. Moody, in my opinion, is often considered one of the greatest communicators of the Gospel and I recently read one of my favorite Moody quotes about the learning curve of Moses... After all, Moses ended up having a fairly decent impact for God!

*"Moses spent 40 years thinking he was somebody;*
*40 years learning he was nobody; and 40 years*

*discovering what God can do with a nobody."*
D.L. Moody [6]

I have to adjust the numbers for my life, but it seems I spent 40 years thinking I was somebody and twenty years learning I was nobody apart from the grace of God. I now am looking at (fill in the blank someday) years praying and seeking to see what God can do with a "nobody". This is not about groveling in self-loathing. Far from it. It is simply acknowledging the liberating recognition of my dependence and need for God.

All of us have a purpose… and a simple lesson I learned regarding purpose came from one of my canine friends out on the farm named Jack. Jack was a black lab we all loved who understood who he was and lived out that identity every day. Jack was predestined to love water, run, and retrieve. That is the destiny of any Labrador Retriever. Jack didn't try to be anything else. Even as a puppy, he chased anything we tossed his way and eagerly brought it back. We did not have to spend one minute training him. It was as natural as breathing for Jack. Retrieving was his purpose and passion. That was the lesson of the day from my four-legged mentor.

All of us have also been created with a purpose. In fact, every person has a God-designed destiny whether they believe it or not. Far too often we just don't fully realize that we are sent to fulfill God-given tasks. We act as if we were simply dropped down in creation and must decide how to entertain ourselves until we die. But we were sent into the world by God, just as Jesus was. Once we start living our lives with that conviction, we will soon know what we were sent to do. Living out who you are is liberating.

The apostle Paul had some thoughts about such a life when he wrote to the church at Ephesus…

*"For it is by grace you have been saved, through faith—and this is not from yourselves, it is the gift*

*of God— not by works, so that no one can boast.
For we are God's handiwork, created in Christ
Jesus to do good works, which God prepared in
advance for us to do" (Ephesians 2:8-10).*

Think about that! You were rescued from the death of sin
by grace. It was a gift that could not be earned. And you are
a new creation, indeed a masterpiece for whom good things
were planned from the beginning of time. The irony of God's
plan is that we become important when we quit thinking we are
important. God can do amazing things with "nobodies" who
are trusting and willing.

Now here's the thing... we all know some students will
show up terrified this year because they have scars and hurt.
Some will wear those scars externally, but most will be hidden.
They'll be concerned about acceptance, about friendships and
about simply getting through the year. They'll be dealing with
stuff at home that they don't talk about, and no one even knows
about. And it's not just students who might struggle. New families and new teachers will arrive with anxiety wondering how
they fit in, wrestling with self-doubt and loneliness.

Loneliness can feel like the worst thing in the world, and it
is something we all, at one time or another, endure. Loneliness
can manifest itself in a variety of ways. Someone can be surrounded by crowds of people or with their family and friends
and still feel lonely. The reasons can be numerous — whether
they feel like they don't belong in that group, going through
a season of change they feel the people around them won't or
can't understand. Or loneliness is when we are physically alone,
and no one is around us. Some people find themselves isolated
through no fault of their own.

There is loneliness felt when someone desires to be loved
by a romantic partner and that answer to prayer is delayed.
It can be amplified when surrounded by happy couples, witnessing their love, wedding photos, and vacations spread all

over social media. It can be felt when someone is childless, longing to be a parent and sees their friends having healthy, happy babies. There are so many ways and reasons to feel lonely, and in those moments, life can seem hopeless, dark, and sometimes not worth living. That is a lie from the enemy!

Loneliness is a tricky emotion. On the one hand, what you feel is totally validated. No one can take away your feelings. On the other hand, loneliness, if left to fester, can lead to false ideations and actions that can be harmful. Loneliness can also cause us to bottle up what we are feeling. The lie that this feeling tells is that no one knows but us is going through this and that no one will ever understand. But when we have the courage to reach out to others, we will certainly find that we are not alone in our feelings — that someone else feels the exact same way.

Although we may feel lonely and are not ready to share with anyone how we feel, we are still never truly alone. There is One who promises to be with us always. When Jesus ascended into heaven, leaving his disciples, his friends — he didn't leave them alone, he left them with someone who would never leave them, someone who would live inside them forever — the Holy Spirit.

> *"So do not fear, for I am with you; do not be*
> *dismayed, for I am your God. I will strengthen*
> *you and help you; I will uphold you with my*
> *righteous right hand" (Isaiah 41:10).*

Throughout Scripture, God promises us that He is with us — we do not have to be afraid or feel hopeless.

That's when you and I show up. We don't need a formal parade to make our students, families, friends, and teachers feel welcomed and loved. We just need a heart that remembers what it was like to struggle, what it was like when someone reached out and what it was like to experience that profound impact in our lives.

We have a chance daily to make others feel welcomed and loved. We have an opportunity to remind them that they matter and that their life is a gift. It might, in fact, be the most important thing they learn this school year! Don't miss the chance to teach it to them today. Today is your day. Live inspired… and maybe, just maybe, that is your purpose!

### An Encouraging Attitude:
Throughout Scripture, God promises us that he is with us — we do not have to be afraid or feel hopeless.

### A Spiritual Insight:
*"So do not fear, for I am with you; do not be dismayed, for I am your God. I will strengthen you and help you; I will uphold you with my righteous right hand"* Isaiah 41:10.

### *A Step to Consider:*

We have a chance daily to make others feel welcomed and loved. We have an opportunity to remind them that they matter and that their life is a gift. It might, in fact, be the most important thing they learn this school year! Don't miss the chance to teach it to them today. Today is your day. Live inspired... and maybe, just maybe, that is your purpose!

# Reflection 5

# *"When Life Gets Blurry, Adjust Your Focus!"*

*October 8, 2022*

*You need to be content with small steps. That's all life is. Small steps that you take every day so when you look back down the road it all adds up and you know you covered some distance. And when life gets blurry, you need to adjust your focus and take those small steps leading toward that goal, whatever it may be!*

I just returned from a visit with my 96-year-old mother. Always treasure those visits these days. Brings back so many memories of my days growing up on our farm. I talked to mom about my memories of walking through the front door on the farm and smelling what she was cooking in the kitchen, and the fact that I then knew I was home. I'm guessing you probably have as well. I recently read that psychologists and brain experts claim the sense of smell is closely linked with memory. In fact, it is more so than any of the other senses. My favorite smell from mom's kitchen was the smell of freshly baked bread after it had just been taken out of the oven. Oh my, they really should make a perfume called "freshly baked bread"!

Mom also did amazing things while preparing meals in her slow cooker, which she often referred to as her crockpot. I've tried to apply some of her cooking methods as I prepare meals, unfortunately, not always the same results...; O) Mom's beef stew was another of those favorite smells of mine that emanated from her "crockpot", and it brought to mind some thoughts I'd like to share in today's reflection.

Many of us, including myself, may be feeling some heat and pressure or experiencing disappointment or constraints with regards to many of the things going on around us in our world these days... Not sure about you, but I've been in that environment many times. I see an analogy here, and I think we can learn a lot from what happens to meat when it is placed in a crock pot for an extended period of times.

Being placed in a crock pot, or slow cooker forces the meat into a confined environment where heat will be applied. The heat brings out the meat's natural juices. The juices then marinate the roast causing the meat to tenderize and produce flavors and smells that draw you in. Afterwards, you get to sit down to a great feast and enjoy the meal with others. "Crock potting" in my opinion is well worth the wait!

The "crock pot" analogy lays out a formula that makes sense to me... Heat, pressure, disappointment, and constraints may add up to create a wonderful outcome in our lives as we face the challenges that may come our way. For each of us, the heat, pressure, disappointment, and constraints may take on a different look. But take comfort. The heat and pressure may be pulling things (juices) out of you that you do not even realize. You just may even become a more tender (compassionate) and inviting person.

John Piper once said, "God is doing 100 things in your life. You might be aware of three of them." So, if you are feeling heat or pressure and experiencing disappointment and constraints, choose joy. You might just be in God's leadership crockpot. Never forget, food tastes better coming out of a crockpot than a microwave... As the political season is again upon us, remember, "crock potted" leaders are better than microwaved ones as well!

This week, the Major League Baseball regular season came to a close. For 20 of the 30 teams, there will be no game tomorrow. It's the end of a journey that started seven months and roughly 190 games (if you count spring training) ago. Like every journey, though, it can only be taken one step at a time. The best teams understand this, and rather than look at the result, they focus on each individual day. They have a process that they follow, a routine that helps get them through the long grind and keeps the season from overwhelming them mentally. You don't have to be a professional athlete to benefit from this approach.

Each of us have goals and things we want to accomplish, and maybe the road to get there looks just as daunting (or even more so) than a seven-month baseball season. I have discovered that my best chance for success lies in taking steps, no matter how small, towards that goal each day.

Some days it won't feel like you're making much progress and that's when you need to trust the process. Because tomorrow you're going to show up and take another step and then another. Eventually you're going to look up and realize just how much distance you've covered! You need to be content with small steps. That's all life is. Small steps that you take every day so when you look back down the road it all adds up and you know you covered some distance. And when life gets blurry, you need to adjust your focus and take those small steps leading toward that goal, whatever it may be!

25

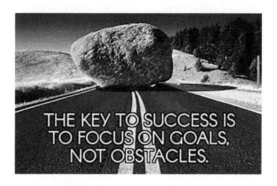

To close out my thoughts today, I was recently listening to a song from my younger days, (been a while ago, so please bear with me) called *"The Games People Play"* by Joe South. I'm finding I'm listening to more music from my younger days which was generally, as a time, pretty turbulent. As I listen to the comments of young people today, I realize that not much, if anything, has changed since this song was recorded in the late 60's. Imagine that!

First two stanzas are as follows – Feel free to sing along...

> *"Oh, the games people play now, Every night and every day now, Never meaning what they say now, Never saying what they mean...*
>
> *And they wile away the hours, In their ivory towers, Till they're covered up with flowers, In the back of a black limousine."* [7]

I must admit that a bit of the anger and power of the protest was diminished with the following hard-hitting chorus...

> *La-da da da da da da da La-da da da da da de, Talking 'bout you and me, And the games people play!*

I know my generation thought we could change the world by promoting love, hope and peace. I see the same anger directed at my generation (pretty much deserved) that we felt toward my parent's generation back in the day. I now often read how this generation is going to change things by promoting love, hope and peace. Can you say full circle?

We are a country divided today, as so many people are placing their hope for happiness on political candidates and parties. I do believe that leaders make a difference and I care deeply about making an informed and prayerful choice. But I never place my hope or desire for change on a politician. I have many friends who are politicians on both sides of the aisle, and I hope they take no offense to my thoughts today.

Did you know the word hope is used about 80 times in the New Testament? The first appearance of the word in the NIV translation pretty much lays out my belief.

*"In his name (Jesus) the nations will put their hope." Matthew 12:21*

Paul wrote about the hope that I have in his letter to the Romans. It reads.

*May the God of hope fill you with all joy and peace as you trust in him, so that you may overflow with hope by the power of the Holy Spirit. Then you will overflow with confident hope through the power of the Holy Spirit. Romans 15:13*

The second chorus of South's tune also has a real pearl of wisdom...

*"God grant me the serenity, to remember who I am."*

27

That is what I have learned as I have faced the "crock pot" challenges of life. I try to remember who I am. A servant who is humbled by God's amazing grace. I think if everyone kept this in mind, it would tone down the rhetoric. My peace lies in the belief that I have hope that is real. I have peace that transcends circumstance. Because of those truths, I can deal with the rest of the news. No matter what happens in in the coming months and years, I am convinced that the following statement is true. God is in control. And that is where my hope rests today!

### An Encouraging Attitude:
Heat, pressure, disappointment, and constraints may add up to create a wonderful outcome in our lives as we face the challenges that may come our way. For each of us, the heat, pressure, disappointment, and constraints may take on a different look. But take comfort. The heat and pressure may be pulling things (juices) out of you that you do not even realize. You just may even become a more tender (compassionate) and inviting person.

### A Spiritual Insight:
*"In his name (Jesus) the nations will put their hope." Matthew 12:21*

### A Step to Consider:
Each of us have goals and things we want to accomplish, and maybe the road to get there looks just as daunting (or even more so) than a seven-month baseball season. I have discovered that my best chance for success lies in taking steps, no matter how small, towards that goal each day.

# Reflection 6

# *"Be an Encourager!"*

*October 23, 2022*

*As a cancer survivor, I have done my best to continue sharing encouragement, inspiration and support for others who may be facing not only serious health issues such as cancer, but other life challenges as well since my cancer diagnosis in 2009. Please consider being an encourager by helping donate to Hope Lodge of Iowa City as the American Cancer Society is now ready to assist Hope Lodge in reopening the facility by sponsoring a fundraising drive to begin serving those in need of a place to stay while being treated for cancer.*

I was blessed to be a part of the Hope Lodge Heroes Campaign Kickoff this past week in Iowa City! Hope Lodge and the

American Cancer Society were instrumental in providing me a place to stay throughout my treatment regimen following my cancer diagnosis in 2009 and helped remove much of that huge financial burden from our family.

Hope Lodge has been impacted by the pandemic as all of us have, and as has been their legacy, they have made the best of the current situation. In response to the COVID-19 pandemic, the American Cancer Society suspended Hope Lodge in Iowa City operations in March 2020, because they could no longer ensure the health and safety of their immune-compromised cancer patient residents, volunteers, and staff. Until it can safely host patients again, the American Cancer Society has offered Hope Lodge facilities as free temporary housing for health care workers who are unable to return home for fear of exposing their families to the coronavirus. They also launched a Response Fund to raise funds to operate their repurposed Hope Lodge facilities during the COVID-19 crisis.

The American Cancer Society is now ready to assist Hope Lodge in reopening the facility by sponsoring a fundraising drive to begin serving those in need of a place to stay while being treated for cancer. This once again touches my heart and is why I'm interested in being involved in helping with this fundraising effort.

By helping with this effort, the Hope Lodge Heroes Fundraiser will assist both cancer victims as well as their caregivers and will provide a needed boost to those in need while allowing those involved to be an encourager in someone else's life, just as the staff and patients at Hope Lodge were for me!

I would appreciate your consideration in donating to this worthy cause. Please find below a link that will take you to the American Cancer Society site where your donation will be received for this worthy project. I'm supporting the American Cancer Society, and you can too!

https://secure.acsevents.org/site/
STR?fr_id=103154&pg=personal&px=47124722

As a cancer survivor, I have done my best to continue sharing encouragement, inspiration and support for others who may be facing not only serious health issues such as cancer, but other life challenges as well since my cancer diagnosis in 2009. Please consider being an encourager by helping donate to Hope Lodge of Iowa City for this worthy cause!

The three books in this series (*Reflections from the Home Team... Go the Distance, Reflections from the Home Team... STAYING POSITIVE When Life Throws You a Curve!* and *Reflections from the Home Team... Reframing the Curveballs Life Pitches Your Way!*) include reflections sharing an encouraging attitude, a spiritual insight, and a step to consider which are frequently blended with baseball analogies and metaphors. Life's challenges are not easy, just as baseball isn't always easy.

The game provides many lessons about success and failure, and those lessons can often be applied in our life journeys. As life's curveballs and challenges come our way, I encourage reaching out to our "Home Teams" both human and divine for the strength, love, support, and comfort needed to meet them.

*"Each of us should please our neighbors for
their good, to build them up." Romans 15:2*

***https://www.reflectionsfromthehometeam.com/***

**An Encouraging Attitude:**
As a cancer survivor, I have done my best to continue sharing encouragement, inspiration and support for others who may be facing not only serious health issues such as cancer, but other life challenges as well since my cancer diagnosis in 2009. Please consider being an encourager by donating to the American Cancer Society.

31

## A Spiritual Insight:
*"Each of us should please our neighbors for their good, to build them up." Romans 15:2*

## A Step to Consider:
The game of baseball provides many lessons about success and failure, and those lessons can often be applied in our life journeys. As life's curveballs and challenges come our way, I encourage reaching out to your "Home Teams" both human and divine for the strength, love, support, and comfort needed to meet them.

# Reflection 7

# *"Extinguish the 'Thought Bubbles' of the Past!"*

*November 6, 2022*

*So often our minds are racing ahead to the next task or worrying about the future. It becomes easy to get overwhelmed or sometimes even scared about what may lie ahead.... Other times we're living in the past regretting something we did or didn't do, and we can get sad and melancholy. I find it comforting that when I live in the present, and extinguish those*

*thought bubbles, I can find peace. It's really the only moment*
*we can do anything about...*

A good friend recently shared the picture I've chosen for this post, and it vividly reminds me of some time I recently spent "dog sitting" with my daughter and son in law's new puppy, Teddy. The picture is a photo of a man and dog sitting on a bench looking out over a forest. There are multiple thought bubbles above the man's head. He's thinking about money, cars, a vacation he might take and his house. There is just one thought bubble above the dog's head. It's filled with the same view he is currently looking at. The caption reads: *"This is why the dog is happier."*

So often our minds are racing ahead to the next task or worrying about the future. It becomes easy to get overwhelmed or sometimes even scared about what may lie ahead... Other times we're living in the past regretting something we did or didn't do, and we can get sad and melancholy.

I find it comforting that when I live in the present, and extinguish those thought bubbles, I can find peace. It's really the only moment we can do anything about. Having had the opportunity recently to spend time with Teddy helped remind me that living in the present can help clear my mind of all those distractions. Living in the present with Teddy helped simplify life along with the many thoughts it was sending my way. It helped me focus on loving those who are close to me, unconditionally, and without distraction.

Another thing that came to mind is the value of relationships in our lives and the importance of not taking those relationships for granted. A quote I recently read from Samuel Johnson put that in perspective for me. It reads:

> *"To let friendship die away by negligence and*
> *silence is certainly not wise. It is voluntarily to*

*throw away one of the greatest comforts of this weary pilgrimage." Samuel Johnson* [8]

It is so easy to take relationships and friendships for granted, something I've worked hard not to do since cancer. Those relationships have helped carry me through some difficult times, and I'm very grateful for them. Just one of the many reasons for me to regularly share my heart with you through my writing.

Often, we may not think we need to tell someone how we feel about them because "they should just know." Maybe that's true but stop for just one moment to consider how much reaching out to someone in your life to thank them for their friendship might mean to them. Can you spare a few minutes (in the present) to send a text/email, or even better, a quick phone call? It will make a huge difference in their day and take just a small investment of time from you. An investment that will surely pay dividends when you realize how much it meant to them. Moving forward, work at simply picking out just one person in your life to reach out to each day and encourage them. It will surely have a positive impact on them.

A popular phrase in our culture these days is, "Life just wears you down." I don't think that's completely accurate. I know our bodies age and eventually give out, but I often hear that phrase uttered by people who are young and physically healthy. So, what gives?

Most of the time, in fact almost always, what wears us down is our thoughts and not our actual activities. How many conversations will go on in your own head today with people you are upset with? How often will you stew about someone else's behavior at work today? How often will you check Facebook and be annoyed at the fact that it looks like other people are having more fun than you?

With midterm elections just around the corner, how often will you visit a news site and get frustrated about something going on in the world of politics or someone's opinion on it?

It's no wonder we feel tired by the end of the day. It's amazing we're even able to get through the day without our heads exploding...

For me, it is important to get clear in my mind on what I can and cannot control. Then act on the things I can control by living in the present. I've found it best to let go of the things I can't control as quickly as possible. When I catch myself having a conversation in my head for the thousandth time with someone who has hurt me in the past, I try to simply remind myself to come back to the present, take a deep breath and shift my focus to something else...

I've also found it helpful to be aware of just how often I'm not living in the present in my life. When I catch myself worrying about the future, or cursing the past, I gently remind myself to get back to the present and the task that is right in front of me.

> *"Therefore, do not worry about tomorrow, for tomorrow will worry about itself. Each day has enough trouble of its own." Matthew 6:34*

The Good News...Don't worry about the things that haven't happened yet. Live in the moment and leave your worries for tomorrow.

### *An Encouraging Attitude:*

Can you spare a few minutes (in the present) to send a text or email, or even better, a quick phone call? It will make a huge difference in their day and take just a small investment of time from you. An investment that will surely pay dividends when you realize how much it meant to them. Moving forward, work at simply picking out just one person in your life to reach out to each day and encourage them. It will surely have a positive impact on them.

## A Spiritual Insight:

*"Therefore, do not worry about tomorrow, for tomorrow will worry about itself. Each day has enough trouble of its own."*
Matthew 6:34

## A Step to Consider:

I've found it helpful to be aware of just how often I'm not living in the present in my life. When I catch myself worrying about the future, or cursing the past, I gently remind myself to get back to the present and the task that is right in front of me.

# Reflection 8

# *"If you're happy and you know it...tell your face!"*

*December 11. 2022*

**Be the reason somebody
smiles today.
Even if it means
just being there.**

*"If You're Happy and You Know It...Tell
Your Face!"*

*Dave Burchett*

If you're happy and you know it... tell your face! Maybe not quite what you were expecting today? Did you start to sing the little song that we often teach kids in Sunday School? I did when I first read Dave Burchett's commentary on the topic. He is one of my favorite authors because he often combines a touch of humor with some serious thinking.

In one of his recent musings, Dave referred to a Charles Schultz image of Charlie Brown's sister Sally struggling to spread frozen butter on her toast. Finally, she exclaims, "Nobody told me life was going to be this hard!" [9]

My experience is that life can often be a journey of struggling to spread frozen butter and sometimes even worse, much worse. Many of us may be going through one of those "frozen butter" times right now, but I have come to understand that those times are part of the journey. God has given us a wonderful gift that we too often leave unwrapped. The gift of laughter. I believe, as Dave does, that a sense of humor is one of God's gifts to help get us to the finish line. Humorist Dave Barry puts it this way... "No matter what happens, somebody will find a way to take it too seriously." [10]

An examination of the life of Jesus would indicate that He too possessed a sense of humor. The writers of Scripture did not set out to author a joke book, so you won't find the phrase "a Sadducee, a Pharisee and a Roman walk into a bar." Clearly Jesus knew how to interact warmly with others and connect with those around Him. And He knew where to find those who needed the touch of forgiveness the most, so often bringing a smile to their face.

Part of any healthy and dynamic group relationship is having fun together. I experienced that this morning at our worship service at Nazareth. We had wonderful music, and a powerful message by our Junior High Ministry Director Derek Akers. It was titled *Hope in the Heartache...* The combination of music and a strong message brought a smile to my face. Derek focused his message on the story of John the Baptist after he was imprisoned. John asked: does God have a plan for the heartache in my life? Where is God in all of this? Do my expectations and reality line up? As a reply in Matthew 11: 4-6 we are reminded of who Jesus is and what He has done in the past...

Jesus replied, *"Go back and report to John what you hear and see: The blind receive sight, the lame walk, those who have leprosy are cleansed, the deaf hear, the dead are raised, and the good news is proclaimed to the poor. Blessed is anyone who does not stumble on account of me." Matthew 11: 4-6*

Troubles don't change the identity of who Jesus is… We need to continue to trust God, even in the face of challenges because God remains faithful, loving and full of Grace despite our heartache. Jesus is the Hope in our Heartache! That should bring a smile to everyone's face!

A lack of humor in the church apparently has been a problem for a while now. Teresa of Avila prayed this simple prayer in 1582, "From somber, serious, sullen saints, save us Oh Lord." A good reminder that is certainly relevant today. The wisdom of Proverbs speaks to us here…

*"A glad heart makes a happy face; a broken heart crushes the spirit." Proverbs 15:13*

Each one of us is unique and needed in God's community. But we often don't feel or live that way. Part of the problem is comparing our talents and gifts to others. There is a long list of gifts I wish I had, but I am uniquely me. Can often lead to what I call a "long face." Being content with who I am really is a heart issue, grounded in the truth of who I am according to Scripture. My fears about my shortcomings are confirmed when I log into Facebook and see the smiling perfection of others. We are psychologically wired toward comparisons and social media is exactly the wrong medicine for that predisposition.

Can we trust Jesus enough to drop the perfection ruse? Can we trust him enough to be authentic? Not needy and demanding. Just honest and real in community and, of course, with Him. I like to think that the fellowship of believers should be the one place where honesty is encouraged. Where shortcomings ought to be accepted. Church should be the place where you can say without fear, "I am struggling, I hurt, I need help." The fact that God created us with a desire to be in community tells me that part of His plan is for us is to be helped by other members of the body of Christ.

So, when someone achieves or creates something that you wish you had accomplished, don't shrink in comparison. Approach them. Celebrate them. Thank God for their contribution. And remember that you also have a vital part in His plan. Writer John Mason wrote these words which I think sums things up pretty well!

*"You were born an original. Don't die a copy."* [11]

We are uniquely and completely designed for our role in this world, let's approach it with a smile. So, let's all join in that familiar Sunday School song...If you're happy and you know it, Tell your face. If you're happy and you know it, Tell your face. If you're happy and you know it, Then your face should really show it. If you're happy and you know it Tell your face!

### An Encouraging Attitude:
We are uniquely and completely designed for our role in this world, let's approach it with a smile. So, let's all join in that familiar Sunday School song...If you're happy and you know it, Tell your face. If you're happy and you know it, Tell your face. If you're happy and you know it, Then your face should really show it. If you're happy and you know it Tell your face!

### A Spiritual Insight:
*"A glad heart makes a happy face; a broken heart crushes the spirit." Proverbs 15:13*

### A Step to Consider:
"You were born an original. Don't die a copy."

# Reflection 9

# *"The Tie That Will Unite Us as Christians?"*

## *January 22. 2023*

*Be kind to unkind people because they need it the most!!*

Today's reflection is intended for a very specific audience… ME! Feel free to "listen in" as I share today's thoughts… Many thanks to author Dave Burchett for his inspiration!

As I was watching last week's Monday Night Football game as a chance to take a break from what had been a very busy and stressful week prior, all that busyness and stress became meaningless as I watched the terrifying collapse of Buffalo Bill defensive back Damar Hamlin. It was obvious from the players reactions on the field that this was not a typical injury situation. We learned that CPR was being administered to restore Hamlin's heartbeat. Millions united in prayer as he was rushed to the hospital in critical condition. I was very much encouraged by the unity shown by people around the world as they joined in prayer and support for Damar and his family while the professionals present worked to revive Damar. Damar's prognosis is very encouraging, and it reminds me that the power of prayer works!

I was once again reminded of the uncertainty of my days on earth... I may have 15 years or 15 minutes to continue my earthly journey, and only God knows that number. Time and time again over the years I have had similar moments where I was reminded to be more aware of how precious life is and to live out of that mindset. A cancer diagnosis can do that! But I always tend to forget and allow myself to fall back into reacting to meaningless annoyances and worthless distractions. Here is my takeaway from the incident on the field in Cincinnati last week.

Every day is sacred... I started running that through my mind each morning this past week and throughout the day. I was driving in Chicago last week on my way home from a visit to the Windy City when a large truck cut me off in the middle of a driving rainstorm (in January no less) and I had my normal "not kind" initial reaction. I don't think that momentary reaction is necessarily sin, at least I hope not because I've had my share of those in my life.

Dwelling on that feeling and allowing it to change my spirit may lead me down a dark path where I definitely don't want to travel. As I remembered my morning emphasis, it reminded me that every day is sacred. That reminder allowed me to change my focus to the bigger picture. I am healthy and able to drive. God protected me from an accident. I don't know what that driver's story might be. So, I simply breathed a short prayer for that driver's safety and those around them. What a difference that awareness made.

Our life journeys are full of frustrating situations and frustrating people. But I believe with all my heart that there are sacred moments to be found in even the most mundane of days. Let me share a disclaimer that I am not accomplished in this practice, but I am praying that the Spirit of God will allow me to recognize these sacred events.

Whether I acknowledge it or not, God is the middle of everything I do. This week's mental post-note is very simple... *Today Is Sacred.* David wrote about the constant presence of God in Psalm 139.

> *"You go before me and follow me. You place your hand of blessing on my head. Such knowledge is too wonderful for me, too great for me to understand! (Psalm 139:5-6, NLT)*

If I believe that to be true, then I must believe there are daily sacred moments to be received and given away. They don't have to be earth shaking in their scope. Just a simple act of love, kindness, service, or concern can be a sacred moment. I don't want to live in a world of frustration, angst, and division.

We witnessed with the reaction to Damar Hamlin's crisis how empowering unity can be. Why can't we as the body of Christ do better? I want to focus on who unites us. *Jesus.* I want to focus on what gives me strength and courage. God's constant presence. I want to pray for open eyes to see and enjoy the sacred moments in every day.

My experience has been that we have groups of fervent believers who choose different visions of where we as a culture, and yes, even where we as Christians should travel on our life journeys. The analogy I like to use is the picture of two railroad tracks which run parallel to each other, never coming together as they travel to their destination. Even though they don't physically join each other on their journey, they are united along the way by the ties that hold them together providing safe passage until a destination is reached. I pray that we can see that tie that holds us together as Jesus and His never-ending love for each of us. We can come together as a culture, and as a country, and yes even as Christians that are experiencing division if we use Jesus's love for us as the "tie" to bring us together and not be divided.

David concludes Psalm 139 with this amazing request...

*"Search me, O God, and know my heart, test me, and know my anxious thoughts. Point out anything in me that offends you and lead*

*me along the path of everlasting life. (Psalm 139:23-24, NLT)*

I try to remind myself that through God's Spirit today and every day is sacred. Let us use that spirit as an instrument to show our love and grace to each other every day. And when we feel emotions, don't fight them, let them wash over us and pass. They are only temporary. Just like in life, we can't force things, but we can find a way to move forward together using Christ as our ultimate and divine tie... It might even include being kind to unkind people because they need it the most!!

### An Encouraging Attitude:
Our life journeys are full of frustrating situations and frustrating people. But I believe with all my heart that there are sacred moments to be found in even the most mundane of days. Whether I acknowledge it or not, God is the middle of everything I do. This week's mental post-note is very simple...*Today Is Sacred.*

### A Spiritual Insight:
*"Search me, O God, and know my heart, test me, and know my anxious thoughts. Point out anything in me that offends you and lead me along the path of everlasting life. (Psalm 139:23-24, NLT)*

### A Step to Consider:
I try to remind myself that through God's Spirit today and every day is sacred. Let us use that spirit as an instrument to show our love and grace to each other every day. And when we feel emotions, don't fight them, let them wash over us and pass. They are only temporary. Just like in life, we can't force things, but we can find a way to move forward together using Christ as our ultimate and divine tie... It might even include being kind to unkind people because they need it the most!!

# Reflection 10

# *"Never Forget Who That One Person May Be in Your Life!"*

*February 5, 2023*

*"Don't walk behind me; I may not lead. Don't walk in front of me; I may not follow. Just walk beside me and be my friend."*

***Albert Camus***

As Super Bowl Sunday draws near, the picture I headline this reflection with stopped me from thinking football for a bit and put things in perspective for me last weekend. The game was the Kansas City Chiefs vs. the Cincinnati Bengals who were playing for the AFC Championship last Sunday for those who don't follow football. The player, Bengals linebacker Joseph Ossai, who drew a costly penalty that allowed Kansas

City the opportunity to move into field goal range and kick a game winning three-pointer to beat the Bengals 23-20.

To me, this is life, and I felt it... Joseph definitely made a costly mistake with his penalty. Thousands (if not millions) of people saw it, got upset and walked away from him (including his teammates). The fans left him... his teammates went to the locker room, coaches left him... hurting. They literally left him on the battlefield alone. I know some of you know this feeling. BUT there was one... One person that refused to leave his brother no matter what happened. He picked him up. *NEVER forget who that one person may be in your life!* They are worth more than gold. THAT'S leadership, that's a friend, that's a brother.

This situation brought to mind a quote from Albert Camus, a French novelist/philosopher whom I've at times referred to when dealing with the life challenges that have come my way. I have often found some much-needed encouragement in his words. It reads:

> *"Don't walk behind me; I may not lead. Don't walk in front of me; I may not follow. Just walk beside me and be my friend." Albert Camus* [12]

Being a good friend to others is important and most of us try our best to treat our friends with kindness and give them the support they need. Here are some things we usually do not say to our friends: You're a loser. You're a failure. You're never going to be successful. You shouldn't even try to do (fill in the blank) because you won't reach it. Why do you even bother trying?

Yet, we often talk to ourselves like this... I know I have. How many times have you said one of the above statements, or something similar, to yourself? Being your own best friend seems like a touchy-feely/new age kind of thing to say, but ask yourself this question: Why in the world should you talk, or treat yourself worse than you would a good friend?

Some people think that if they are hard on themselves, it will push them to perform better. Really? Do you feel more motivated at work by a boss that constantly criticizes you and tells you you're no good? Or do you work harder and perform better for one who encourages you even when pointing out areas you could improve on?

Sure, sometimes I'll admit I can be a mess. Cancer has played with my mind so many times... The Pharisees were a great example of tidy people trying to make tidy clones. Because they didn't identify as sinners, they had no need for a Savior.

They were tidy. Healthy. Self-righteous. And they had no time for Jesus and His love for messes.

As Luke 5:31 states:

> *"It is not the healthy who need a doctor but the sick."*

Jesus was very clear. He called people to repentance and told them humility is being able to admit they are sick. Humility is saying we need help; we can't do it on our own. We are terminally ill. When we recognize just how sick we are, persistence kicks in. Think about this physically: Once we know we're sick, we call for that doctor's appointment. If there's nothing available, we insist and even become impatient. We'll call and call and call, hoping to be squeezed in. It was no different with Jesus.

Some of us may believe we can't come to Jesus until our life is all tidy. We may think Jesus isn't going to have anything to do with us until we clean up our mess. This isn't true. The Good News is better than that: Jesus can't do anything for you until you admit you're a mess. Admitting that we're a mess is the repentance Jesus was talking about.

As for those friends who stick by us along the way while we clean up our messes, we need to remind ourselves to carve our name on their hearts, not our tombstones. Our legacy will be etched into the minds of others and the stories they share about us.

Most of us will not have buildings named after us or become famous for a historic scientific discovery. But we all can live on in the hearts of those we love. And really, what could be better than that?

Let's keep in mind that it is the hearts that we touch and the lives we enrich that will be our deepest and most meaningful legacy. The most important thing in life is people, not things.

### An Encouraging Attitude:
"Don't walk behind me; I may not lead. Don't walk in front of me; I may not follow. Just walk beside me and be my friend." Albert Camus

### A Spiritual Insight:
*"It is not the healthy who need a doctor but the sick." Luke 5:31*

### A Step to Consider:
Let's keep in mind that it is the hearts that we touch and the lives we enrich that will be our deepest and most meaningful legacy. The most important thing in life is people, not things.

# Reflection 11

# *"Looking UP to Where Our Help Comes From..."*

*February 25, 2023*

*Today's world events and uncertainties can often bring waves of hopelessness into our daily lives... For me, the movie, 'A Man Called Otto' highlighted the importance of community and a shared sense of belonging during challenging times that forced Otto (Tom Hanks) to continue living. Watching Otto grapple with moments of hopelessness and self-doubt that weighed heavily on his conscience tugged at my heartstrings. My tears were worth it though... All in all, the movie felt like a warm hug from a dear friend...just what I needed!*

This past weekend I took in a movie titled "A Man Called Otto" starring Tom Hanks. The movie is a fable of 63-year-old Otto (Tom Hanks) a widower wrestling with grief after losing his wife to cancer. Otto would like you to believe that he's a 21st-century Scrooge. A stickler for rules, he scoffs at neighbors who do not sort their garbage and keeps their pets at arm's length. Like the machines he dearly loves, Otto is mechanical with his routine and is cautious with his emotions.

What I took away from the movie was a humanizing experience by a group of misfits who were learning that getting along can also be lifesaving. Otto repeatedly strives to insulate himself from the people around him and plots to die by suicide until his new neighbors move in and one by one spoil his plans.

Marisol, an immigrant mother of two adorable daughters and a wife to Tommy, an IT guy, forces Otto into situations that need him to extend empathy and love — from asking him to become her driving instructor to turning him into a babysitter at her convenience — her spirit cracks Otto's hard exterior. The movie challenged me to leave my pessimism at the door and embrace the "old grumpy man" in myself.

Today's world events and uncertainties can often bring waves of hopelessness into our daily lives... For me, the movie, 'A Man Called Otto' highlighted the importance of community and a shared sense of belonging during challenging times that forced Otto to continue living. Watching Otto grapple with moments of hopelessness and self-doubt that weighed heavily on his conscience tugged at my heartstrings. My tears were worth it though... All in all, the movie felt like a warm hug from a dear friend... just what I needed!

The movie brought back this past summer's memories of sitting at my favorite fishing hole here in Cedar Falls, a place I usually go to enjoy some solitude and stillness as well as the simple beauty of nature. While leaning back in my chair, a flock of eight Canadian Geese noisily left the lake, landed on shore near me and waddled toward me. They lined up and "honked" expectantly. If I spoke their language, I suspect the translation would have been something like the famous quote from Caddyshack... "Hey, how about a little something, you know, for the effort, you know."

I fed the geese part of my sandwich and apparently that was an acceptable offering. Each time I go back to my spot, the geese would waddle over and wait for their snack. I was fascinated by their behaviors. They always stayed together. There was a clear leader of the pack and when the leader decided it was time to move on to other activities the seven dutifully followed. They swam at the same time. Groomed at the same time. They slept at the same time. They were created to thrive in community. So are we...

We were created to be in a community with other believers. Because of our unity in Christ, we are to embrace those different from ourselves. That's what makes a church dynamic to a person who experiences grace and acceptance for the first time. And that is why church can be devastating when a congregation becomes selective, judgmental, and legalistic.

Anne Lamott shares a thought-provoking observation that speaks truth for me:

> *"You can safely assume you've created God in your own image when it turns out that God hates all the same people you do."* [13]

55

That is both an ouch and an amen statement. When differences result in judgment, what we thought was a safe place instead becomes the biggest betrayal of all. When we become "experienced" Christians, something seems to happen. We can lose touch with our former brokenness and sinfulness and desperate need to be forgiven and accepted. That is when the pretense begins that our holiness is based on performance instead of complete dependence on Christ.

Sadly, life can include disappointments, losses, and heartaches. Because it does, when they happen, it can cause a sense of hopelessness when they seem to affect what we thought was going to be our future. Overnight it can feel like we have no future and all our hopes and dreams have been shattered. Just what I perceived Otto to be experiencing in the movie after the loss of his wife to cancer...

Lately, wars and rumors of wars fill our headlines, along with reports of natural disasters impacting people's lives, our food sources, fuel supplies, and mobility. Yet, Jesus urged us in Matthew 24:6 not to be alarmed.

> *"You will hear of wars and rumors of wars but see to it that you are not alarmed. Such things must happen, but the end is still to come."*
> Matthew 24:6

Because life's uncertainties seem on the increase, where can we find hope when what we've hoped for and planned seems to be passing away? As Christians, we can turn to God, who is unshakable, unmovable, and everlasting, in whom we can put our future hope and trust in without fear.

Still, in an ever-changing world, it may be hard for us to wrap our heads around this truth. We've become conditioned to having the rug pulled out from under us at a moment's notice. Yet with God, we can have confidence He is for us, knowing

He seeks to fulfill the desires of our hearts and to give us what we ask and need. A verse in Matthew 7:7 comes to mind.

> *"Ask and it will be given to you; seek and you will find; knock and the door will be opened to you." Matthew 7:7*

As we move forward in the upcoming year, let's not focus on the situations and circumstances surrounding us that can bring feelings of hopelessness and despair, but rather, look up to where our help comes from.

> *"The Lord will keep you from all harm—he will watch over your life; the Lord will watch over your coming and going both now and forevermore." Psalm 121:7-8*

Let's leave our pessimism at the door while embracing the "old grumpy man" in ourselves as we move forward in loving and caring community. Together, while trusting our Father's faithfulness, we can look to the future with positivity and hope as we delight in each other's company making it a priority that no one ever feels alone.

### An Encouraging Attitude:
Because life's uncertainties seem on the increase, where can we find hope when what we've hoped for and planned seems to be passing away? As Christians, we can turn to God, who is unshakable, unmovable, and everlasting, in whom we can put our future hope and trust in without fear.

### A Spiritual Insight:
*"The Lord will keep you from all harm—he will watch over your life; the Lord will watch over your coming and going both now and forevermore." Psalm 121:7-8*

*A Step to Consider:*

Let's leave our pessimism at the door while embracing the "old grumpy man" in ourselves as we move forward in loving and caring community. Together, while trusting our Father's faithfulness, we can look to the future with positivity and hope as we delight in each other's company making it a priority that no one ever feels alone.

# Reflection 12

# *"Leadership is a Life of Service"*

*March 12, 2023*

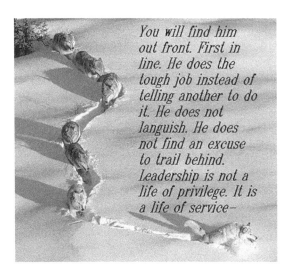

You will find him out front. First in line. He does the tough job instead of telling another to do it. He does not languish. He does not find an excuse to trail behind. Leadership is not a life of privilege. It is a life of service–

*This world needs good servant-leaders. Servant leaders love others. In fact, this is the defining element of servant leaders– If we truly love those who we may have the opportunity to lead, then we cannot help but treat them well. We will do right by them. Doing the right thing is not always the easy thing, often the right thing is the complicated, messy, and even hard to do thing, but we do the right thing, nonetheless.*

Well, Spring Break has arrived, and Major League Baseball is in full swing with Spring Training games preparing all those players hopeful of making a Big League Roster. It is a special time of year, not only for those players, but for the families who enjoy kicking back and enjoying a relaxing day at the ballpark!

I was visiting with a friend this past week and the subject of why Americans like baseball came up. She was not born in the States and doesn't quite get baseball. That conversation gave me the opportunity to put into words some ideas of why I love baseball. And now, that's given me a topic for this blog post.

The cheering, the laughter, and the sheer enjoyment that everyone feels at a ballpark is almost intoxicating. You can't help but catch on and feel the buzz. There are many reasons to enjoy baseball: the excitement of a HR; the beauty of a double play; the amazing skill of chasing down a fly ball in the outfield. And if you are at a live game, forget about it! The beauty of the ballpark is worth the ticket in itself. But one shouldn't feel that they have to like baseball... It's one form of beauty and enjoyment among the endless assortment of human activities and endeavors worth admiring and enjoying. For me however, it goes much deeper than that.

Baseball has allowed me to develop many friendships and partnerships with some amazing people over the years. What strikes me is how many of those folks have used their 'station in life' to reach out to others who may be in need, leading by example as they serve others. One such example is George Springer, who currently plays for the Toronto Blue Jays, formerly a member of the Houston Astros, 2022 World Champions. In the face of a multitude of global problems, it can be difficult to feel like an individual or small groups can make a difference. Our minds and hearts are often in the right place, but what can one person really do? It turns out quite a lot...

I ran across a story recently about George and a young boy named Mateo Sanchez. They share a speech disorder disability, stuttering. Mateo is a huge baseball fan, and George is his idol. They were brought together back in 2017, and the meeting and continued friendship and support by George since has helped Mateo not only work through his disability but also spread his message about overcoming the challenges stuttering poses, especially in the life of a young teenage boy which can be difficult at times, even without such a disability. [14]

Mateo has been making presentations to other young people about stuttering turning a difficult diagnosis into a message of hope for other young people thanks to the guidance and inspiration George has provided. This summer, Mateo has plans to work on a public service announcement about stuttering awareness to help kids like him. The pair has stayed in touch since 2017, and they've watched each other grow from afar. A few weeks ago, they reunited at Spring Training. It is a heartwarming story and can be viewed at this video link which played recently on the MLB Network…

https://www.youtube.com/
watch?app=desktop&v=skfoDPUJjQI

Mateo doesn't wonder how to get past the stutter anymore. He owns it. It's part of his identity, but it's not who he is. He's a big brother, a loving son, a jokester, a baseball player, and a friend to many other young people. Sure, he still feels the sting of rude remarks and that hurts. He can just handle it better now thanks to the inspiration and support George has provided. Maybe Mateo will continue to improve his stutter and grow out of it, maybe he won't. Either way, Mateo has grown into it, and he's perfect just the way he is.

The message I want to share with today's post is twofold... First, we need to accept each other despite our differences or disabilities, just a Christ accepts each of us...

In this passage from Romans Paul writes:

> *"Accept one another, then, just as Christ accepted you, in order to bring praise to God." Romans 15:7*

Secondly, just as George Springer reached out to Mateo, leading with his friendship and support while providing the inspiration and motivation for Mateo to help overcome his disability, may each of us use every opportunity we are granted to become servant leaders and do the same. As this verse in Matthew points out...

> *"Not so with you. Instead, whoever wants to become great among you must be your servant." Matthew 20:26*

This world needs good servant-leaders. Servant leaders love others. In fact, this is the defining element of servant leaders — *they lead with love, just as George has done with Mateo.* If we truly love those who we may have the opportunity to lead, then we cannot help but treat them well. We will do right by them. Doing the right thing is not always the easy thing, often the right thing is the complicated, messy, and even hard to do thing, but we do the right thing, nonetheless.

Jesus taught His disciples that servant leadership was the prescribed form of leadership for the Kingdom of God. Then he modeled it! He modeled it by loving them. He modeled it by teaching them, by being patient with them, by washing their feet, and ultimately by going to the cross for them and for us.

I offer up this prayer today as we head into spring and all the blessings it brings our way...

> *Lord, scripture reminds us that you do not discriminate based on gender, race, economic status, disability, or background. I pray that Jesus helps us all to see people just as He sees them, looking past the physical and into their hearts. Let us all welcome people with open arms, minds, and hearts with people who may look and think differently from us. Give us discernment as we seek to honor you in everything we say and do. Forgive us when we fall short. We love you and thank you for your patience as we navigate life in a fallen world. Amen.*

### An Encouraging Attitude:

The message I want to share with today's post is twofold... First, we need to accept each other despite our differences or disabilities, just a Christ accepts each of us... Secondly, just as George Springer reached out to Mateo, leading with his friendship and support while providing the inspiration and motivation for Mateo to help overcome his disability, may each of us use every opportunity we are granted to become servant leaders and do the same.

## *A Spiritual Insight:*

*"Not so with you. Instead, whoever wants to become great among you must be your servant." Matthew 20:26*

## *A Step to Consider:*

Jesus taught His disciples that servant leadership was the prescribed form of leadership for the Kingdom of God. Then he modeled it! He modeled it by loving them. He modeled it by teaching them, by being patient with them, by washing their feet, and ultimately by going to the cross for them and for us.

# Reflection 13

# *"Every Day Can Be Like Opening Day!"*

*April 9, 2023*

*It is Opening Day, or Opening Week in this case, and every team is looking up and looking ahead for hope… Each fan has dreams too, and they are hopefully, or perhaps hopelessly, optimistic. Last year's disappointments are gone and the hope of a new season dawns for thirty-six thousand fans in the park and thousands more across the area. The mood is upbeat and the expectations high. May we all experience an 'Opening Day' renewal each and every day!"*

I had a chance to take in a ball game in St. Louis this past week between the Atlanta Braves and the St. Louis Cardinals.

Even though it wasn't opening day, it felt like it to me... In my mind there is no more special day in sports than 'Opening Day' in baseball. The smell of freshly cut emerald green grass delights the senses. The base lines are painstakingly and perfectly defined by a grounds crew that is committed to perfection on this day.

The players act like little boys. On this day these athletes appear extra grateful that they are paid to play a kid's game. Children skip school and parents do not care because memories are being made for both.

Souvenirs are treasures to be kept a lifetime. The atmosphere is truly magical!

The hot dogs taste like gourmet food—they should for what they cost!

All of this happened for me at Busch Stadium this past week!

It is Opening Day, or Opening Week in this case, and every team is looking up and looking ahead for hope... Each fan has dreams too, and they are hopefully, or perhaps hopelessly, optimistic. Last year's disappointments are gone and the hope of a new season dawns for thirty-six thousand fans in the park and thousands more across the area. The mood is upbeat and the expectations high.

This is a new day and a new season. Old mistakes are forgotten. Past errors are no longer important. Today is the annual renewal of the incredible marathon that is big league baseball. It is a clean slate. The team has a new identity.

I was thinking about this at this morning's Easter Service, funny how the mind can drift at times... sorry Pastor Mike. For me, the example of "Opening Day" can also be a reminder about our walk with Jesus. Recently I have often been reminded that God's Word tells us that every day can be like Opening Day...

I do have a clean slate because of Christ. There is hope. Yesterday's sins are forgotten if you have accepted the gift of Jesus on the Cross. As a cancer survivor, every morning that I awake and see the magic of a new sunrise I can believe that I have been renewed and optimistically face the day. I don't have to wait a year to have a chance for renewal.

In Romans 12, Paul writes that every day has the potential for the spiritual magic of renewal and victory in Christ. Paul lays out a 'game plan' on how to achieve this magical renewal...

> *"If your gift is serving others, serve them well.*
> *If you are a teacher, teach well.*
> *If your gift is to encourage others, be*
> *encouraging.*
> *If it is giving, give generously.*
> *If God has given you leadership ability, take*
> *the responsibility seriously.*
> *And if you have a gift for showing kindness to*
> *others, do it gladly.*
> *Don't just pretend to love others. Really*
> *love them.*
> *Hate what is wrong. Hold tightly to*
> *what is good.*

*Love each other with genuine affection and
take delight in honoring each other.
Never be lazy but work hard and serve the
Lord enthusiastically.
Rejoice in our confident hope. Be patient in
trouble and keep on praying.
When God's people are in need, be ready
to help them. Always be eager to practice
hospitality.
Bless those who persecute you. Don't curse
them; pray that God will bless them.
Be happy with those who are happy, and weep
with those who weep.
Live in harmony with each other. Don't be
too proud to enjoy the company of ordinary
people. And don't think you know it all!
Never pay back evil with more evil. Do things
in such a way that everyone can see you are
honorable."
Romans 12:7-17 NLT*

Paul's words give me hope as we face the many challenges confronting all of us these days. I am grateful in my spiritual journey that God has given me a chance for an "Opening Day" renewal every day. I have had some down seasons during my "career" as a follower of Jesus. But I have learned that every day is a gift! I realize that every day with Jesus can be like this special day in baseball.

I can believe that hope for the future is real. I can understand that I must be a better teammate to others that I encounter and not expect my team to be perfect. The magic of a fresh start happens once a year in baseball. It can happen any day and every day for a follower of Jesus.

We can find that hope by attending church services while listening and interacting with others interested in experiencing that same hope in a community of believers… I read a post this morning shared by a friend which speaks to my heart in this regard. It reads:

> *"If you still are on the fence about going to church this weekend for Easter, I want to encourage you to go.*
>
> *A perfect church doesn't exist. A perfect pastor doesn't exist. A perfect congregation doesn't exist. So don't worry about trying to find one.*
>
> *Just go. Show up as you are—no matter the junk you may have in your life.*
>
> *If you've never been inside a church, no one will even know this weekend. Churches will be full of new faces, and they will welcome you with open arms.*
>
> *You don't have to have an Easter dress. You don't have to have a new outfit. You don't need to have it all together. You don't have to have all the answers. Just go.*
>
> *You are never too far gone for Jesus. Every single church is full of humans who are flawed but faithful, broken but believing, imperfect but inspired. People who may be hanging on by a thread, but grace keeps them hanging in there.*
>
> *So, if you are still thinking about it—just go.*
>
> *You will be welcomed.*
>
> *By the people.*
>
> *But most importantly, by Jesus."* [15]

May we all experience the "Opening Day renewal" Christ offers us each day!

### An Encouraging Attitude:

I can believe that hope for the future is real. I can understand that I must be a better teammate to others that I encounter and not expect my team to be perfect. The magic of a fresh start happens once a year in baseball. It can happen any day and every day for a follower of Jesus.

### A Spiritual Insight:

*"If your gift is serving others, serve them well.*

*If you are a teacher, teach well.*

*If your gift is to encourage others, be encouraging.*

*If it is giving, give generously.*

*If God has given you leadership ability, take the responsibility seriously.*

*And if you have a gift for showing kindness to others, do it gladly.*

*Don't just pretend to love others. Really love them.*

*Hate what is wrong. Hold tightly to what is good.*

*Love each other with genuine affection and take delight in honoring each other.*

*Never be lazy but work hard and serve the Lord enthusiastically.*

*Rejoice in our confident hope. Be patient in trouble and keep on praying.*

*When God's people are in need, be ready to help them. Always be eager to practice hospitality.*

*Bless those who persecute you. Don't curse them; pray that God will bless them.*

*Be happy with those who are happy, and weep with those who weep.*

*Live in harmony with each other. Don't be too proud to enjoy the company of ordinary people. And don't think you know it all!*

*Never pay back evil with more evil. Do things in such a way that everyone can see you are honorable."*

*Romans 12: 7-17 NLT*

*A Step to Consider:*
You are never too far gone for Jesus. Every single church is full of humans who are flawed but faithful, broken but believing, imperfect but inspired. People who may be hanging on by a thread, but grace keeps them hanging in there. So, if you are still thinking about it—just go. You will be welcomed. By the people. But most importantly, by Jesus."

# Reflection 14

## *"Listen, and Honor Other's Stories..."*

*April 23, 2023*

*"When you have the opportunity to talk to someone who opposes your opinions/thoughts/ points of view, you should ask to hear their story. Why do they have such strong feelings? Did something or someone cause that reaction? It is amazing how hearing someone's story can often soften our hearts toward them..."*

**Dave Burchett**

S pent some time in Iowa City a week ago with some follow up appointments. Overall, I was comfortable with the reports. While the news was encouraging, a conversation taking place that I was sitting next to, between two individuals waiting "their turn" became quite loud and animated...

The thing that truly troubled me as I sat and listened is how the conversation progressed from a casual conversation about the current status of each of their health situations to a series of intense exchanges ranging from several current social issues to each person's faith walk (or lack of it). Let's just say it wasn't good.... It was quite obvious they were on opposite ends of the spectrum regarding their stance on all of the issues.

Wow... I'm glad I had my most recent reading project along *"In Order to Live"* by Yeonmi Park to help occupy myself while waiting. (It is a great read that puts a lot of things in perspective for me). Yeonmi is a North Korean refugee who escaped North Korea with her mother to China, where they were betrayed and sold into slavery before making their way to Seoul, South Korea. Her testimony is heartbreaking and unimaginable, but never without hope! It is a story about the human spirit that we can all learn from, especially when we tend to take for granted the freedoms we enjoy in this country! I highly recommend it.

Getting back to that conversation in Iowa City, one of the things that I struggle with the most in our current cultural climate is the broad brushing of people by all sides. I've found that far too often, if there may be a disagreement with someone's faith or political views, they many times tend to be automatically assigned the worst values from the most extreme people proclaiming that particular message. Without knowing a single thing about their story, their heart, or their background, many times they tend to get thrown down the gauntlet of judgment.

When I witness the initial judgment of others without knowing that other person's heart, I have often asked myself what the best way to deal with that might be... Honestly, it reminds me of the Last Supper Jesus had with his disciples but more specifically, it makes me think about Judas.

Jesus knew Judas was going to betray Him and Jesus knew exactly what that betrayal meant… Yet, even still, Jesus broke the bread and drank the wine with Judas. He shared with Judas the first and most Holy Communion KNOWING that it would also be the last Passover meal he would ever participate in. Jesus then knelt before all the disciples, including Judas, and then washed their feet. Jesus didn't exclude Judas and he didn't run Judas out of the Passover meal.

Instead, Jesus washed the feet of the man who would send him to the Cross. As far as Jesus was concerned, "hating the sin" and "loving the sinner" didn't mean mocking Judas, calling Judas names, being angry toward Judas, excluding Judas from a holy dinner or posting a cruel meme about Judas on social media.

So, what should be our response to such attacks? Well, I think Jesus made what should be our response pretty clear in the 5th Chapter of Matthew.

> *"You have heard the law that says, 'Love your neighbor' and hate your enemy. But I say, love your enemies! Pray for those who persecute you! In that way, you will be acting as true children of your Father in heaven. For he gives his sunlight to both the evil and the good, and he sends rain on the just and the unjust alike. If you love only those who love you, what reward is there for that? Even corrupt tax collectors do that much. If you are kind only to your friends, how are you different from anyone else? Even unbelievers do that." Matthew 5:43-47, NLT*

> "When you have the opportunity to talk to someone who opposes your opinions/thoughts/

75

points of view, you should ask to hear their story. Why do they have such strong feelings? Did something or someone cause that reaction? It is amazing how hearing someone's story can often soften our hearts toward them..." Dave Burchett [16]

I have listened to many stories on my cancer journey and now have a much better understanding of why people tend to react the way they do. And listening (really listening) can open a door to dialogue about your own journey and story. You will be acting as a true child of God by having that conversation!

By owning our failures, we acknowledge that we all fall short... In the movie *The Jesus Revolution* (a wonderful movie I recently took in that I would also recommend) a Church welcomed in young men and women who were doing drugs and living a life that many in the congregation deemed decadent.

If the message had been clean up your life and then you can be part of our community, the revival would have stopped cold. Instead, the message was come to know Jesus and let Him show you how to change how you live. That happened millions of times during that remarkable revival. It can still happen today. But my concern is that God cannot use us if we are busy broad brushing everyone we disagree with. I want to share His story without judging theirs, so I am throwing away the broad brush! May we all consider doing the same.

### An Encouraging Attitude:

I have listened to many stories on my cancer journey and now have a much better understanding of why people tend to react the way they do. And listening (really listening) can open a door to dialogue about your own journey and story. You will be acting as a true child of God by having that conversation!

### A Spiritual Insight:

*"You have heard the law that says, 'Love your neighbor' and hate your enemy. But I say, love your enemies! Pray for those who persecute you! In that way, you will be acting as true children of your Father in heaven. For he gives his sunlight to both the evil and the good, and he sends rain on the just and the unjust alike. If you love only those who love you, what reward is there for that? Even corrupt tax collectors do that much. If you are kind only to your friends, how are you different from anyone else? Even unbelievers do that." Matthew 5:43-47, NLT*

### A Step to Consider:

If the message had been clean up your life and then you can be part of our community, the revival would have stopped cold. Instead, the message was come to know Jesus and let Him show you how to change how you live. That happened millions of times during that remarkable revival. It can still happen today. But my concern is that God cannot use us if we are busy broad brushing everyone we disagree with. I want to share His story without judging theirs, so I am throwing away the broad-brush! May we all consider doing the same.

# Reflection 15

# *"If You Don't Have Hope, You Don't Have Anything."*

*May 6, 2023*

*"If I work hard," I think I can. If you don't have hope, why do you even get up in the morning? If you don't have hope, you don't have anything."*

*Kasumba Dennis*

Baseball scouting is an interesting line of work… I recall a baseball game I was recently attending to observe a position player who had been recommended to me. As he walked to home plate in his first at bat, this particular player stood and watched three pitches cross the heart of the plate without ever swinging the bat... The pitcher wasn't throwing hard, these were not breaking balls... These were "fastballs," if I would dare use that word.

The young man in the batter's box I was there to observe certainly looked the part. He had the wrap-around shades, the elbow guard, the shin guard, the Evo Shield wristbands, and the "baserunner's mitt" (designed to protect the hand of someone sliding into a base) rolled up and sticking out of his back pocket. He waggled the bat and scraped the bottom of his cleats across the dirt as he stepped in the box. But three perfect pitches later he was retreating to the dugout! I couldn't help but shake my head after I watched him strike out having never swung the bat and I thought to myself, "Swing the bat!"

I've often wondered if God says the same thing to me from time to time. I wonder if I look the part and say the right things but miss the opportunities God may have waiting for me because I am just happy to play the game... and that brings me to today's reflection.

I often hear lots of excuses when things may not go well on a given day for a player I may be observing as a baseball scout. To all those athletes who think they need all the high-priced training equipment and top of the line facilities in order to be successful... I say work ethic comes first. The rest will follow no matter what the conditions are that you work in.

A former teammate and friend recently shared a story with me about a young man from Uganda who has a dream and the hope of playing professional baseball, a dream that many young athletes aspire to here in the United States. So, I did a bit of research and give credit to Kevin Baxter, a sports columnist from the Los Angeles Times for sharing the story of Kasumba Dennis, an 18-year-old who grew up in an orphanage as so many children do in his home country of Uganda.

That hope feeds Kasumba's big league dream, in a country where just 2,500 people are estimated to be playing the game, and on a continent that has produced just two major leaguers. To quote Kasumba, "If I work hard," I think I can. If you don't have hope, why do you even get up in the morning? If you don't have hope, you don't have anything."

Paul Wafula, Kasumba's coach found him in a slaughterhouse. By the time he was 14, hunger and hopelessness had led Kasumba to drop out of school and take a job slaughtering cows, sheep, and goats. It was a harsh environment, one in which the workers, mostly young boys, were bathed in blood.

Wafula remembered the pair's first conversation: "I asked him why he was working in the slaughterhouse, and he was like, 'I want to have something to eat. We don't have anything to eat at home.'"

So Wafula, a volunteer baseball coach, made the boy a deal: leave the slaughterhouse and each time he came to the baseball field he'd get fed. When Kasumba became a regular, Wafula sweetened the deal: if he kept coming, the coach would pay for him to go back to school too. And so began a relationship that would confirm Wafula's belief in the redemptive power of the sport and fill Kasumba, now 18, with dreams of becoming Uganda's first major leaguer.

Wafula and Kasumba are an odd couple, one formed by necessity and forged with determination. For the coach, who is perpetually upbeat, his default expression is a warm gap-toothed smile. He shares that Kasumba is proof that Uganda's oft-forgotten orphans can aspire to more than a desperate existence in a slaughterhouse. For the player, who is often stoic and quiet, already worn down by his life experiences, Wafula feeds those aspirations from a bottomless well of encouragement, inspiration, and faith. Wafula, who at 28 is just ten years older than Kasumba, is more life coach than baseball coach, one who speaks in affirmations and believes deeply that sport can change lives, because it changed his.

Like most children in Uganda, he played soccer before changing to baseball, starring for the Uganda national team after playing five seasons as a pitcher and outfielder with an independent league team in Japan. Yet it's his failures more than his successes that inform the lessons he teaches his players. "I was once living in the ghetto. I don't want the same situation to happen to these kids because when they have nothing to occupy themselves, they have different groups to join," he said, referring to neighborhood gangs.

Wafula's classroom is a bumpy field owned by a local church in Gayaza, a dusty, crowded crossroads about 15 miles from the center of Kampala, Uganda's capital. There is an uneven dirt infield, two dugouts, a tiered concrete grandstand behind a flimsy wire backstop, and just the hint of a pitcher's mound. Herds of cows and long-horned Ankole cattle make frequent trips through the outfield looking for places to graze — and leaving behind cow pies that make diving catches treacherous.

No one there is sporting the wrap-around shades, the elbow guard, the shin guard, the Evo Shield wristbands... but rather sporting the internal drive and work ethic that Coach Wafula is inspiring in those young players!

Kasumba and his grandmother share a tiny brick-and-stucco house with seven others. Hidden down a narrow, rutted dirt road, the house has a concrete floor and no furniture or running water. A single, bare light bulb dangles from a cord in the center of each of the house's three rooms and the air is thick with stench from the cow pens less than 50 yards from the front door.

This is the reality Kasumba hopes to escape through baseball. So, each morning, he pushes himself off a thin mattress just as the sun begins to peak over the horizon. The day will unfold just as the last one did, and the one to follow. Kasumba will step into the muddy path in front of the house and perform a dizzying array of drills using, among other things, a stack of old tires, plastic bottles filled with water and a weathered blue backpack stuffed with rocks.

When Coach Wafula talks about developing players, he really means developing people. If the orphans on his team never play on a bigger stage than the ragged field in Gayaza, at least they have a zinc roof over their heads, some food in their stomachs and someone who cares about them. And if Kasumba never makes it to the U.S., much less the major leagues, all that work will not have been in vain. He's learned to have hope through the discipline, compassion, and dedication he has internalized under the tutelage of Coach Paul. He will be a success, whether in baseball or in life given the lessons he has learned!

Kasumba's inspiring story is well documented on Ben Verlander's podcast at the following link, it's truly a must see as Kasumba has recently been accepted into the Major League Draft League where he can pursue his hopes and dreams!

https://www.foxsports.com/watch/play-65d895db4001544

I've been with the Atlanta Braves Organization since 1989, and the organization recently unveiled the City Connect uniforms, where the greatest Brave of all-time was honored in the design. Under the bill of the cap is the phrase, Keep Swinging. This is a nod to one of Hank Aaron's famous quotes:

> *"My motto was always to keep swinging. Whether I was in a slump or feeling badly or having trouble off the field, the only thing to do was keep swinging." Hank Aaron[17]*

And that's what God wants us to do. Keep swinging. Don't be complacent. Don't get discouraged. Don't become cynical. There's a difference between knowing and doing. Keep swinging, and trust that the Holy Spirit will be working in and through you, despite your circumstances or perceived roadblocks.

Just as Coach Wafula has inspired Kasumba to work hard at overcoming his circumstances while pursuing his dream, we need to remind ourselves that even though difficulties and challenges abound in this world, we can rejoice that Jesus is always present to help us cope with any and all circumstances, knowing that all things are possible with him.

> *Jesus looked at them and said, "With man this is impossible, but not with God: all things are possible with God." Mark 10:27*

Keep swinging!

### *An Encouraging Attitude:*
Just as Coach Wafula has inspired Kasumba to work hard at overcoming his circumstances while pursuing his dream, we need to remind ourselves that even though difficulties and challenges abound in this world, we can rejoice that Jesus is always present to help us cope with any and all circumstances, knowing that all things are possible with him.

*A Spiritual Insight:*
*Jesus looked at them and said, "With man this is impossible, but not with God: all things are possible with God." Mark 10:27*

*A Step to Consider:*
"My motto was always to keep swinging. Whether I was in a slump or feeling badly or having trouble off the field, the only thing to do was keep swinging." Hank Aaron

And that's what God wants us to do. Keep swinging. Don't be complacent. Don't get discouraged. Don't become cynical. There's a difference between knowing and doing. Keep swinging, and trust that the Holy Spirit will be working in and through you, despite your circumstances or perceived roadblocks.

# Reflection 16

## *"Life Is About Adjustments!"*

*May 29, 2023*

*"I've learned that to succeed in life, just as in baseball, along with the challenges both may pitch our way, we must be able to make adjustments. If your plan isn't working, adjust your plan and Never Give Up! Yes... life and baseball truly are about making adjustments!"*
**David Welter**

A cancer diagnosis impacts many parts of your life – whether you have just found out you have cancer, are getting treated, or have finished treatment. You likely feel both the physical and emotional changes which can impact the way you feel and how you live. Having cancer can also make many feelings seem more intense. These feelings may change daily, hourly, or even minute to minute. This is true whether you're currently in treatment, done with treatment, or the friend or family member of someone with cancer. These feelings are all normal...

I've found that talking about your cancer can help you deal with all the emotions you may be feeling. Letting your family and friends know about your diagnosis is important as it may affect them as much as you. The people in your life may also feel worried, angry, or afraid. My perspective towards life and throughout this journey was always one focused on positivity and encouragement which had been modeled for me by what I called my "Home Team" (both human and divine). I don't think I could have made it without my family, my students, staff, and those I interacted with in Iowa City during my cancer treatments. I think one of my favorite ways of describing the experience came from a quote by Yogi Berra, one of my all-time favorite baseball "characters". "Baseball is 90% mental; the other half is physical..." Oh how that applies to the cancer journey!

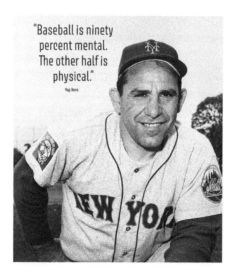

The cancer journey is a constant struggle between mind and body... Even though Yogi may have had his numbers a bit off, his point is well taken. I've learned that to succeed in life, just as in baseball, along with the challenges both may pitch our way, we must be able to make adjustments. If your plan isn't working, adjust your plan and Never Give Up! Yes... life and baseball truly are about making adjustments!

Making ourselves available to others can open the doors of opportunity for deeper relationships, healing, and transformation. For many, time is one of the most valuable commodities in today's fast-paced world. Sharing time with others is a wonderful gift. It says, *"Here I am... for you. To listen, to care, to serve."* The power of presence should never be underestimated!

I truly believe that God didn't save me from something, but rather, he saved me FOR something. I made up my mind that I was going to reach out to others who were struggling with cancer personally or with their loved ones who had supported them during their cancer journey with the same positivity and encouragement I had received. I was going to do whatever I could to provide them with support and encouragement. It was time to give back!

To do that, I created a blog, titled *"Reflections from the Home Team"* to share bimonthly messages of positivity and encouragement. It can be accessed at this link if interested: ***https://reflectionsfromthehometeam.blogspot.com/***

I had many individuals encouraging me to turn those reflections into a book, which I did. The title *Reflections from the Home Team* seemed so appropriate for where I am in my life at this time, and since, I have authored three books in the *Reflections from the Home Team* book series.

I am also an active supporter of Hope Lodge in Iowa City and the Relay for Life Committee in Black Hawk County. I was incredibly fortunate to have insurance during my treatments, but the cost of medical care and lodging was financially burdensome. Without the assistance of Hope Lodge, the journey would have been much different and even more difficult.

In addition to Hope Lodge, the American Cancer Society and Relay for Life are extremely important to me. Black Hawk County Relay for Life has graciously recognized me by selecting me as their 2023 Survivor of the Year. The "Relay Event" gives me the opportunity each year to help provide encouragement and support to others, and it also helps recharge my batteries as well.

To give back, I will be donating a portion of all book sales from my website and at this year's Relay Event to the American Cancer Society's Relay for Life in Black Hawk County. I would greatly appreciate it if you would consider purchasing a book from my website for anyone in need of positivity and encouragement. For more information regarding the *Reflections from the Home Team* book series, and to order your signed, personalized copy(s) while also gaining access to the "Home Team" blog, just visit my website at: ***Reflectionsfromthehometeam.com***

My heartfelt thanks are extended to the American Cancer Society and the Black Hawk County Relay for Life for recognizing me as their 2023 Survivor of the year... Life most certainly is about adjustments, and, as one of my favorite coaches always told us, *"It's great to be alive!"*

As a Survivor, I appreciate so much the opportunities I have had to visit with others about the challenges of a cancer journey. It has been an incredible experience sharing heartfelt thoughts with others as we face the physical, emotional, and spiritual challenges of life's journey together...

Whenever faced with challenges, no matter how difficult, it is important to try your best to remain positive. I have made that my life's purpose following my treatments and blessings as a survivor. I will continue to work sharing a message of positivity and encouragement to those who may be struggling with life challenges. Romans 12:12 has provided me with some guidance along the way...

*"Be joyful in hope, patient in affliction, faithful in prayer." Romans 12:12*

God's richest blessings to all as we honor those who have sacrificed to protect the freedoms that so many take for granted on this Memorial Day Weekend!

### *An Encouraging Attitude:*

My heartfelt thanks are extended to the American Cancer Society and the Black Hawk County Relay for Life for recognizing me as their 2023 Survivor of the year... Life most certainly is about adjustments, and, as one of my favorite coaches always told us; *"It's great to be alive!"*

### *A Spiritual Insight:*

*"Be joyful in hope, patient in affliction, faithful in prayer."* Romans 12:12

### *A Step to Consider:*

Making ourselves available to others can open the doors of opportunity for deeper relationships, healing, and transformation. For many, time is one of the most valuable commodities in today's fast-paced world. Sharing time with others is a wonderful gift. It says, *"Here I am... for you. To listen, to care, to serve."* The power of presence should never be underestimated!

# Reflection 17

# *"How Can We Stay Optimistic in a Pessimistic World?"*

*June 11, 2023*

*As I was waiting for the My Waterloo Days Parade to start, I ran into my nephew, Josh who works with the Waterloo Police Department. He was on duty helping everyone enjoy their experience at the My Waterloo Days celebration. I am very proud of him and the work he does serving all of us here in the Cedar Valley. While visiting with Josh, it brought to mind a question that I want to take some time to reflect on, that*

*being... How can we stay optimistic in an ever increasingly pessimistic world? ... the focus of today's reflection.*

I had a wonderful time this past Friday evening at the My Waterloo Days Parade helping represent Black Hawk County's Relay for Life. It was such a great way to celebrate the community as well as well as to enjoy all the smiling faces along the Parade route... and there were a lot of them! I especially enjoyed all the kids and their "puppy dog" eyes longing for a piece of candy to be tossed their way...

As I was waiting for the My Waterloo Days Parade to start, I ran into my nephew, Josh who works with the Waterloo Police Department. He was on duty helping everyone enjoy their experience at the My Waterloo Days celebration. I am very proud of him and the work he does serving all of us here in the Cedar Valley. While visiting with Josh, it brought to mind a question that I want to take some time to reflect on, that being... How can we stay optimistic in an ever increasingly pessimistic world? ... the focus of today's reflection.

I'd like to begin by being completely transparent. I am saddened, frustrated, and very much disappointed with the anger and division in our society today. By solely focusing on divisive issues, it often leads to more anger, fear, and yes, hopelessness. I've tried my best to show a path forward to others who may be experiencing what can so often seem a hopeless situation in the cancer journey, and I see some parallels here.

So how can we be optimistic amidst this societal chaos? As a survivor, when I am feeling down, I often try to find some comfort music... I flip from the depressing news that can often overwhelm us to a list of some classic songs that provide a respite from such depressing news. One of the tunes provides me an answer to the question of how to remain optimistic in the midst of chaos and fear. It's a song titled *"He Lives"* by Nicole Mullen. You can listen to it at the following link if interested.

https://www.youtube.com/
watch?reload=9&app=desktop&v=c798azHfoeI

I am and will continue to be optimistic in this journey because of the belief conveyed beautifully in these lyrics sung by Nicole C. Mullen.

> *Because He lives,*
> *I can face tomorrow.*
> *That's it! Because I believe Jesus lives, I can*
> *face tomorrow.*

The next lyric should be true if I truly believe Jesus lives.

> *Because He lives,*
> *All fear is gone.*

I am not saying that the "evil one" does not try to generate fear in my heart when faced with challenges, and I am certainly not perfect in rejecting those fear attacks. But I am learning to remember every day that God is in control. I remind myself daily that He loves me as His child. He sent His Son to die on a Cross while bearing my sins past, present, and future. Jesus rose from the grave and conquered death. I believe that. And that belief leads to this verse sung by Nicole...

> *Because I know*
> *He holds the future*
> *And life is worth the living*
> *Just because He lives.*

I now try to view every negative event (and there are plenty of them) through that lens of HOPE. This really hits home for me as our theme for this year's Relay for Life is *'Every Step Brings Hope'*...

God holds the future, and the HOPE I carry with me as a survivor each and every day. My life for Him is worth living no matter what trials I will endure. Jesus was pretty clear that our journey with Him would be challenging.

> *"I have said these things to you, that in me you may have peace. In the world you will have tribulation..."*

Jesus didn't say we might have some problems now and then. He honestly said you will have trials and tribulation. Why are we so surprised when that happens? The "evil one" definitely tries to distract us from the rest of His promise.

> *"But take heart; I have overcome the world."*
> *(John 16:33, NLT)*

We need to read the words of Jesus carefully. I have overcome the world. It will be okay. At times the journey will be rough, but we can all believe with all of our hearts that our faith will be rewarded in eternity with Christ.

I know that most of us have to learn the lessons of life the hard way. I am still learning after all of these years how to follow Jesus more consistently. He is so incredibly patient and loving as I stumble along. Because He lives, we can face tomorrow without fear, and life is worth the living just because He lives.

To quote Dave Burchett, one of my favorite writers...

> *"I have written many times that Satan wants us to live in regret of the past or fear of the future. Either strategy robs us of the joy of today. For followers of Jesus the past is forgiven. The future is in His hands. Believing that allows us to live in this moment with gratitude, peace, and joy. Something else that gives me optimism in*

*this fallen world is that I used to believe that my sin caused Jesus to leave my side until I repented and returned to His presence. Now I know He never leaves me in those moments. Through the presence of the Holy Spirit, I have the constant presence of God in my journey. I don't have to do anything except remember my need for forgiveness, grace, and love and turn to His constant presence. He is there always. Ready to encourage, love, and direct my path."* Dave Burchett [18]

May we all face the life challenges that come our way by remembering that every step we take with Jesus at our side brings us hope, knowing full well that He Lives! Wishing everyone a great summer!

### An Encouraging Attitude:
Something that gives me optimism in this fallen world is that I used to believe that my sin caused Jesus to leave my side until I repented and returned to His presence. Now I know He never leaves me in those moments. Through the presence of the Holy Spirit, I have the constant presence of God in my journey. I don't have to do anything except remember my need for forgiveness, grace, and love and turn to His constant presence. He is there always. Ready to encourage, love, and direct my path." Dave Burchett

### A Spiritual Insight:
*"I have said these things to you, that in me you may have peace. In the world you will have tribulation...But take heart; I have overcome the world." (John 16:33, NLT)*

*A Step to Consider:*

May we all face the life challenges that come our way by remembering that every step we take with Jesus at our side brings us hope, knowing full well that He Lives!

# Reflection 18

# *"Running A Relay For Life!"*

*June 14, 2023*

*Dave Welter and Lynette Hockey have been designated as the honorary cancer survivor and honorary caregiver for the American Cancer Society's annual Relay for Life of Black Hawk County event on Friday at Hawkeye Community College.*

S pecial thanks to Melody Parker and the Waterloo-Cedar Falls Courier for highlighting this year's Relay for Life celebration in today's Waterloo-Cedar Falls Courier edition! Lynette and I hope to see you all at Hawkeye Community College this Friday evening to support the cause in fighting cancer! Please find Melody's article below:

Melody Parker writes:

Dave Welter and Lynette Hockey are paying it forward.

They have been named the honorary cancer survivor and honorary caregiver, respectively, for the American Cancer Society's annual Relay for Life of Black Hawk County. The annual family-friendly event is from 4 to 10 p.m. Friday at Hawkeye Community College.

"At our Relay for Life, we share moments of laughter, moments of silence, provide shoulders to cry on or hands to high-five," said Candy Nardini, event coordinator. "We raise funds to help the American Cancer Society develop breakthrough research, provide free lodging to patients and give free rides for treatment."

Survivors, supporters, and others form teams to participate and raise funds at the Relay, while others donate or sponsor the event.

"I was surprised and humbled," said Welter of Cedar Falls of learning he was chosen as the honorary survivor. He was diagnosed with Stage 3 throat cancer on his 55th birthday, Feb. 26, 2009. While undergoing several months of chemotherapy and radiation, he began journaling and blogging about his experiences as a way to cope with cancer.

"It was pretty hard, painful stuff. I ate cottage cheese and applesauce and dreamed about cheeseburgers and steak," said Welter, smiling. He was thrilled when people reached out to him to say that sharing his thoughts provided encouragement and gave strength to others in similar situations.

Later he wrote a series of books with the overall title "Reflections from the Home Team," providing encouragement, spiritual insight, and steps for dealing in positive ways with challenges and discouragement — all using his favorite sport, baseball, as an analogy.

"Baseball can teach all kinds of lessons. Everyone needs encouragement and positivity," explained Welter, now cancer-free. "The diagnosis was a shocker. I hadn't smoked a day in my life." He was told the culprit might have been exposure to farm chemicals. "I was given a 50-50 chance of survival. Six of us came in on the same day for treatment with the same diagnosis. Three of us made it, and three of us didn't. God always has a plan."

Welter retired in 2016 as principal at Holmes Junior High School after 37 years with Cedar Falls Community Schools, including 17 years as the head varsity coach for the high school baseball team. He continues to serve as a Major League baseball scout for the Atlanta Braves.

Hockey, of Evansdale, was the primary caregiver for her daughter, Kelsey Rae Lee, after she was diagnosed at 14 with a rare cancer, Stage 4 synovial cell sarcoma, which had already spread to her lungs.

"It wasn't just me. It was our whole family," said Hockey, including Kelsey's father, Randy, and her sisters Nicole and Stephanie. Other family members and friends "could be counted on to provide support," too. In fact, Kelsey herself started a Relay for Life team — "Team Little Lee" — in 2007 for family and friends.

"We've participated in Relay for Life in some way ever since then," said Hockey. "People sometimes forget that cancer affects more than just the person who is diagnosed. It impacts the entire family."

An athlete at Bunger Middle School, Kelsey fell at a volleyball tournament and developed a hematoma that refused to heal. After her diagnosis, she underwent 13 months of treatments and surgeries. At 16, she was diagnosed with leukemia and underwent a bone marrow transplant. At 18, she was told cancer had returned to her lungs.

Undaunted, Kelsey remained engaged and as active as possible throughout her cancer journey, Hockey said. She was named Prom Queen and graduated from Waterloo East High School, as well as the medical secretary program at Hawkeye Community College. At 22, she lost her battle with cancer on Dec. 31, 2011."Kelsey was fearless. She wanted to be involved.

She was an amazing kid," said her mom, adding that Kelsey is loved and remembered daily. The family continues to live by one of Kelsey's favorite quotes, "Dream as if you'll live forever. Live as if you'll die tomorrow."

Theme for this year's Relay for Life is "Cruisin' for a Cure." Activities include a car show and shine, with the first 50 vehicles to sign up receiving a dash plaque. A freewill donation is requested for registration.

There will be a silent auction from 4 to 8 p.m. with items displayed at Tama Hall, and food will be available from Chickfil-A, Nelly's and Bambino's. A DJ will spin tunes and a children's zone will feature crafts, games, a bounce house and pedal cars from Pedal Time LLC.

The walking track will be illuminated by luminaria bags. Each one represents someone with a story tell. Names on all the bags will be read at a special luminaria ceremony at 8 p.m.

"This is a time for us to grieve those we've lost and a time to reflect on how the disease has touched each of us personally. It's a time to look inside ourselves with quiet reflection and find home," said Nardini.

"Because no matter what our experience with cancer has been, we all share the hope that we will one day live in a world where our children and their children will never have to hear the words 'you have cancer,'" she added.

### An Encouraging Attitude:
"Because no matter what our experience with cancer has been, we all share the hope that we will one day live in a world where our children and their children will never have to hear the words 'you have cancer.'"

### A Spiritual Insight:
*"Be joyful in hope, patient in affliction, faithful in prayer.*
*"Romans 12:12*

## *A Step to Consider:*

This is a time for us to grieve those we've lost and a time to reflect on how the disease has touched each of us personally. It's a time to look inside ourselves with quiet reflection and find home. At our Relay for Life, we share moments of laughter, moments of silence, provide shoulders to cry on or hands to high-five, and we raise funds to help the American Cancer Society develop breakthrough research, provide free lodging to patients, and give free rides for treatment.

# Reflection 19

# *"Who Is Your Favorite Superhero?"*

*July 10, 2023*

*We are all most likely starved for real-life heroes – and I can assure you, we probably aren't alone. So, who's your favorite Superhero?*

I recently had the joy of helping celebrate my grandson's third birthday party here in Cedar Falls … He is all about Spiderman in the world of 2023 Superheroes. I must admit that names like the Green Lantern and Batman came up, however my all-time favorite is Superman!

I don't think Finnegan has been exposed to Superman yet, so when the time is right, I'll make some popcorn and sit down and introduce him and his sister to the movie Superman. I'll just bet they may be humming the Superman theme song as they "fly" back to their house.

The Superhero theme at his birthday party got me thinking of some of the things I took away from the Supermen movie. Superman wasn't just showing me how to fight crime in a fictional world, but also how to serve and lead in the one in which we currently live. Please find below a few lessons from the Superman movie which I took away that may apply to us all.

First, we all long for a hero. Superman operated in a scary and broken world. Reminds me at times a lot of today's world. When something bad happened, people would look around and cry out, "Where's Superman!?" Then, faster than a speeding bullet, he'd arrive to save the day!

Our world can be a scary place, too. At times, friends and family can turn their backs on us flippantly, work and studies can get strenuous, the push to succeed becomes overwhelming, or when simply experiencing true acceptance may seem impossible... At those times, children, and yes, even we as adults need to seek someone we can respect, model, get attention from and give our love to. We may find that attention either with someone else or with each other and it could be either outside of our home or within it. If we get the opportunity, we need to make the time to become that hero in another person's life.

Secondly, doing the right thing isn't always the popular thing. How often I've thought that as a parent, grandparent and yes, as a principal. Superman was always jumping into the middle of perilous situations with walls crumbling, bullets flying and kryptonite draining his strength. While others ran backward, he flew forward.

Frequently we can tend to give into group thinking because of the pressures of social media and our use of technology. We need to be strong enough to move in a different direction, as what may be best for others may not be best for us.

Third, we all need someone to encourage us to fly. One of my favorite scenes in the movie is when Superman arrives on his first date with Lois Lane. Near the end of the date, he takes her flying. Soaring over Manhattan, she was first terrified, then a bit more relaxed and eventually comfortable. He then gently releases his snug hold of her, clasps her hand in his and lets her fly next to him. It's as if she is the one flying.

I remember my first driving lesson as a kid, probably around age seven. My dad took me out in our field on the farm, had me sit in the driver's seat of our Allis Chalmers tractor while sitting on his lap. He was in control of the accelerator, clutch, and brakes, had one hand on the wheel (the other gently guiding my hands): But I was certain I was driving that tractor! He made me feel, not just in driving, but in all things, that I could fly. The world today lifts and celebrates negativity that will stifle our creativity and dreams. Instead, dream big and remember that anything is possible.

And finally, take time for yourself. In the midst of fighting crime, pursuing Lois Lane, moonlighting as Clark Kent and solving the world's problems, Superman would occasionally retreat to his ice castle to recharge before returning renewed.

In the midst of our obligations, it's easy to miss the miracle of the moment and instead become irritated by tasks of the day. It is important to plan time to retreat and refresh. For many this cannot always be a full-blown getaway, but could you steal five minutes to watch a funny video? Rock out to your favorite song? Catch fireflies this evening or wake up ten minutes early to enjoy a sunrise?

We are all most likely starved for real-life heroes – and I can assure you, we probably aren't alone. So, who's your favorite Superhero?

I know who I have turned to when I need some time to retreat and refresh... I often write about the importance of Christian community, and it is there where I have so often found peace and comfort during my times of challenge. Some real-life Superheroes truly do exist there!

I have a hunch as to why Jesus spent so much time with sinners. I think he preferred their company because the sinners were honest about themselves and had no pretense, Jesus could deal with them. In contrast, the "saints" put on airs, judged him, and sought to catch him in a moral trap. In the end it was the saints, not the sinners, who arrested Jesus.

The early church was a mix of all types of people. The reason the faith spread against all odds can be found in this description in Acts...

*"And all the believers met together constantly and shared everything they had. They sold their possessions and shared the proceeds with those in need. They worshiped together at the Temple each day, met in homes for the Lord's Supper, and shared their meals with great joy and generosity– all the while praising God and enjoying the goodwill of all the people. And each day the Lord added to their group those who were being saved."* (Acts 2: 42-46)

I suspect that body of believers resembled quite a motley crew yet made up quite a collection of Superheroes! We were all created to be in this community. A safe place that accepts and embraces those different from us because of our bond in Christ. That is what makes church dynamic to a person who experiences grace and acceptance for the first time. And that is why church can be devastating when the congregation becomes selective, judgmental, and legalistic.

Then Jesus said, *"Come to me, all of you who are weary and carry heavy burdens, and I will give you rest. Take my yoke upon you. Let me teach you, because I am humble and gentle at*

*heart, and you will find rest for your souls. For my yoke is easy to bear, and the burden I give you is light."* (Matthew 11:28-30)
Now there is THE SUPREME SUPERHEROE!

Some days we may feel like Clark Kent. But it's time to remember this truth: you can be Superman or Superwoman too, and the best is yet to come with Jesus at our side!

### An Encouraging Attitude:

Some days we may feel like Clark Kent. But it's time to remember this truth: you can be Superman/Superwoman too, and the best is yet to come with Jesus at our side!

### A Spiritual Insight:

*"Come to me, all of you who are weary and carry heavy burdens, and I will give you rest. Take my yoke upon you. Let me teach you, because I am humble and gentle at heart, and you will find rest for your souls. For my yoke is easy to bear, and the burden I give you is light." (Matthew 11:28-30)*

### A Step to Consider:

I know who I have turned to when I need some time to retreat and refresh... I often write about the importance of Christian community, and it is there where I have so often found peace and comfort during my times of challenge. Some real-life Superheroes truly do exist there!

# Reflection 20

# *"Don't Argue With Reality!"*

*July 30, 2023*

*"When you argue with reality, you lose, but only 100% of the time."*

**Byron Katie**

B aseball is in full swing following the All-Star break, and with it comes the pressures of a pennant race, as well as the frustrations of a season that may not be living up to expectations... With both come the "reality" of whichever circumstance you may be facing. My Atlanta Braves are enjoying a stellar first half, and I'm hopeful it will continue.

111

As that thought crossed my mind this past week, it reminded me of a passage in a book I read a while back called "A Nice Tuesday" written by Pat Jordan. Pat Jordan was a former top pitching prospect, who the Milwaukee Braves gave a then-record $36,000 bonus to in 1959... Peanuts in today's market, but big money then!

He retired after three unsuccessful seasons in the minors and went on to carve out an amazing career not only writing books, but also writing magazine profiles for Sports Illustrated, The New York Times Sunday Magazine and Rolling Stone just to name a few. There was one scene in Pat's book that has stuck with me ever since. Pat wrote about his brother George...

> *"George had gotten old. Not physically but mentally. He had spent all his energy trying to impose his order on the world." Pat went on to then describe a scene where he was helping George carry a chair up to brother's attic and it wouldn't fit. George kept trying to push it and push it. Finally, after measuring the chair and the hallway, Pat realized it wouldn't fit. He gave up and went home. Turns out, George did get the chair through the hallway. How? He sawed the legs off it rendering it useless."*

Pat continued...

> *"Over the years, the world had exhausted my brother. He got tired of sawing the legs off things that didn't fit. So, he stopped trying. He had lost the energy, and the will, to control things. So, he just made his world smaller and smaller and smaller."* [19]

I often see that happen when we feel the need to control everything. When people must behave a certain way to be happy, or the weather must be the way we want it, (maybe at least a little break from the heat??) or the breaks of the game must fall our way. It's exhausting to live that way. It wears us down. And we begin to 'shrink' our lives so that we don't risk getting upset.

As Byron Katie says. *"When you argue with reality, you lose, but only 100% of the time."*[20]

If baseball has taught me anything over the years, it is a common fact that you will not win an argument with the umpire, the "ultimate authority" in a game... believe me, I've tried on occasion.)

So why not stop arguing with reality? Control what we can control – own our individual attitude and approach and understand that the rest of the world most likely isn't going to fall in line with our specifications or always meet our expectations while understanding that Jesus is the "ultimate authority" in our lives.

This thought has really stuck in my mind recently as several close friends and acquaintances have been battling ongoing cancer issues either themselves or with family. I think back to when I was "arguing" with the reality that I had been diagnosed with cancer. It is a tough and ugly reality, and easy one to argue with.

We all have friends, some we may simply call acquaintances, but many of us are blessed with one or two friends with whom we can share our most cherished dreams, as well as our deepest disappointments. These are the people we love and trust, and we would do just about anything for them, and they would certainly return the favor.

Some critics say that Christians often have an agenda and dangerous desire to control other people's lives. I confess that has been true for some "religious types". But the followers of Jesus that I have gotten to know over many decades don't resemble that stereotype at all. Perhaps that is why Jesus warned so plainly about the dangers of power. The selfless, giving, and caring believers get little notice in this world, but I believe they are quietly and faithfully making a difference. Jesus upset the organizational chart by placing those who serve at the top.

It is easy to dismiss the hypocrite, and no problem for me to ignore the angry and judgmental religious types. I could not dismiss or ignore so readily however the joy, peace, strength, courage, and love that so many Christians I have known modeled. I could not ignore them because their lives were authentic and different (different good, not weird). I try hard to be that kind of Christian, not always successful, but I take these words of Jesus seriously.

> *"So now I am giving you a new commandment:*
> *Love each other. Just as I have loved you, you*
> *should love each other." John 15:12*

That was not a helpful suggestion. Jesus made that command the cornerstone of following Him. So that is my agenda. To love others as I have been loved and to be a support and helpful servant to those who may be struggling with hope in the "reality" of their life journey.

### *An Encouraging Attitude:*
As Byron Katie says. "When you argue with reality, you lose, but only 100% of the time." If baseball has taught me anything over the years, it is a common fact that you will not win an argument with the umpire, the "ultimate authority" in a game... believe me, I've tried on occasion.

### *A Spiritual Insight:*
*"So now I am giving you a new commandment: Love each other. Just as I have loved you, you should love each other." John 15:12*

## A Step to Consider:

...So that is my agenda. To love others as I have been loved and to be a support and helpful servant to those who may be struggling with hope in the "reality" of their life journey.

# Reflection 21

# *"Fundamentals...Getting Back to Basics!"*

*August 31, 2023*

*"Legendary Green Bay Packers Coach Vince Lombardi famously began each training camp by gathering his wide-eyed rookies and grizzled veterans around him. He would begin by holding up the pigskin in front of him and solemnly proclaiming an indisputable truth... 'Gentlemen, this is a football.' From that rather rudimentary start he would detail the importance of understanding the fundamentals of the sport."*

**Dave Burchett**

I love football along with the fall season that has just begun. I've learned many valuable life lessons playing the sport in both High School and College, just as I did while playing baseball. The opening of football season allows me to enjoy watching some great athletes getting ready to play a highly skilled game here at the high school level in Cedar Falls.

So, what does the team start with every summer at training camp? Footwork and technique drills! Coaches demanding constant repetition of fundamental skills. The best teams most always are the ones that most consistently execute the most basic, fundamental aspects of their craft, much like spring training in baseball.

Fundamentals are best taught by those who have the gift of teaching and complete knowledge of the skills required. You hope you can find an expert to teach you those fundamentals.

Author Dave Burchett shares that legendary Green Bay Packers Coach Vince Lombardi famously began each training camp by gathering his wide-eyed rookies and grizzled veterans around him. He would begin by holding up the pigskin in front of him and solemnly proclaiming an indisputable truth... "Gentlemen, this is a football." From that rather rudimentary start he would detail the importance of understanding the fundamentals of the sport.

I certainly can learn something from Coach Lombardi's approach with his players in training camp! One of the lessons I have taken from Coach Lombardi over the years was his daily expectation of being on time... To Coach Lombardi, being on time meant you always came ten minutes early to a scheduled meeting or skill session.

That bit of advice has always served me well whether on the job, on the field or battling through cancer treatments which so often felt intense like 6:00 a.m. twice a day conditioning drills in the football pre-season. I can definitively say however that the most important lesson Coach Lombardi taught is the importance of community—a trait that must be a part of

118

any successful team. I have felt that sense of community for many years from my "Home Team" and I am so very grateful for the strength and comfort that team has provided on my life's journey.

In today's culture, I so often see people who are desperate to find community and belonging and they often find it in the wrong places. I see men and women (sometimes boys and girls) lose their lives because they found "identity" in groups that promised family and acceptance but delivered heartbreak and abuse instead. All of us want to find someone who will accept us for who we are.

Over the past several weeks, I have lost several friends to cancer, and it has been difficult to watch those who loved and cared for those individuals grieve their losses. This is where I see the "fundamental of community" come into play.

Psalm 133 provides me a sense of comfort when dealing with grief...

> *"How good and pleasant it is when God's people*
> *live together in unity!" (Ps.133:1, NIV)*

119

There is no community more powerful than a group of believers who live in unity. Nothing levels the playing field like Jesus when we genuinely follow Him. In Paul's letter to the Thessalonians, he offered the benefits of honest community.

*"And we urge you, brothers, admonish the idle, encourage the fainthearted, help the weak, be patient with them al" (1 Thessalonians 5:14).*

That seems like such an important message in today's culture as we contemplate the devastating and heartbreaking impact that grief can take on a person. There is also a toll on us that division exits; not only in our society, but in our Churches.

Interestingly, the challenges from Paul are listed for me from easiest to hardest. I can certainly admonish the idle all day long. I am pretty good about encouraging the fainthearted. On my good days I do my best to help the weak. But be patient with them all? That may be the hardest part for me.

But that is the beauty of community. It can be both messy and beautiful. Both frustrating and fulfilling. It truly is life... And it is best lived together with other messy, beautiful, frustrating, and fulfilling folks who still are quite capable of maybe not being as patient as we should be.

And that tees up the biggest need for the "fundamental" of community as found in Galatians.

*"Dear brothers and sisters, if another believer is overcome by some sin, you who are godly should gently and humbly help that person back onto the right path. And be careful not to fall into the same temptation yourself. Share each other's burdens, and in this way obey the law of Christ. If you think you are too important to help someone, you are only fooling yourself. You are not that important" (Galatians 6:1-3).*

Of course, a loving, caring and supportive community isn't the only ingredient for success, but it's certainly a key ingredient that helps make us, everything we do and everyone around us better. Just as in football, when we learn the fundamentals, the rest of the offense falls into place.

As we get back to the basics, remember He is our Father who loves us and wants the best for us. If the answer is no that is an answer. That can mean our request may be answered later, or it may be answered differently. It may not even be answered at all. But through all those responses we must trust that He is holy, powerful, and present. Let's all embrace that fundamental truth as we continue our life journeys.

### *An Encouraging Attitude:*
Of course, a loving, caring and supportive community isn't the only ingredient for success, but it's certainly a key ingredient that helps make us, everything we do and everyone around us better. Just as in football, when we learn the fundamentals, the rest of the offense falls into place.

### *A Spiritual Insight:*
*"Dear brothers and sisters, if another believer is overcome by some sin, you who are godly should gently and humbly help that person back onto the right path. And be careful not to fall into the same temptation yourself. Share each other's burdens, and in this way obey the law of Christ. If you think you are too important to help someone, you are only fooling yourself. You are not that important" (Galatians 6:1-3).*

### *A Step to Consider:*
As we get back to the basics, remember He is our Father who loves us and wants the best for us. If the answer is no that is an answer. That may mean our request may be answered later, or it may be answered differently. It may not even be answered at all. But through all those responses we must trust that He is

holy, powerful, and present. Let's all embrace that fundamental truth as we continue our life journeys.

# Reflection 22

# *"Hard Things Put in Our Way Call for Courage!"*

*September 10, 2023*

*"Based on a true story, the just released movie THE HILL follows Rickey Hill who dreams of being a professional baseball player. Rickey's story illustrates for me that the human spirit is one of ability, perseverance, and courage that no disability can steal away! It proves that hard things are put in our way, not to stop us, but to call out our courage and strength."*
*David Welter*

A good friend recently recommended to me a wonderful movie titled *THE HILL,* and I'm so glad he did. It was just what I needed given the past few weeks, and the challenges

I have witnessed some close family and friends experience. Warm up the apple pie for your movie nibbles, the ingredients of this sports drama are God, baseball, and "old-fashioned American values."

*THE HILL* is the story of Rickey Hill, the son of a traveling pastor who overcomes several physical obstacles to pursue his dream of playing baseball in the major leagues. Based on a true story, the just released movie *THE HILL* follows Rickey Hill who dreams of being a professional baseball player. Rickey is a natural-born slugger, but a physical disability means that he can't walk without leg braces. His preacher father, Pastor James Hill, wants Rickey to put childhood fantasies away, but Rickey has faith that God wouldn't have given him talent if he wasn't intended to use it.

Rickey's story illustrates for me that the human spirit is one of ability, perseverance, and courage that no disability can steal away! It proves that hard things are put in our way, not to stop us, but to call out our courage and strength. So often, David and Goliath tales are hard to come by these days, but *The Hill,* is one that *hits a home run for me*—in more ways than one. In this case, Rickey Hill's obstacle is not a seven-foot giant. Instead, he faces a degenerative spine disease that threatens both his dreams of playing Major League Baseball and his ability to walk.

To his father, James, Rickey's disability is God's sign to pursue "a higher calling". As James sees it, baseball was a distraction from meaningfully serving God. But even as a small child, Rickey disagrees. What if he truly can serve God through his passion of baseball? (I can relate!)

Having a dream to play Major League baseball is a dream that many young people share, in fact it was one that I grew up with. That dream, along with appreciating the opportunity to serve God and others throughout our life journey is certainly a worthy goal. What we often don't plan on is how rocky and steep the road can be at times. Isn't that how life so often plays out? Unexpected things happen that discourage our hearts.

At times, I have experienced God sending the perfect person, community, or event to get me through a hard time. God's Word can give us direction and light in the darkness. Perhaps the best road map is found in Proverbs.

> *"Trust in the Lord with all your heart; do not depend on your own understanding. Seek his will in all you do, and he will show you which path to take." Proverbs 3:5-6*

The big lesson I took away from *THE HILL was* that perseverance, hard work and trust in God and His plan for our lives got Ricky the opportunity to achieve his lifelong dream. The reward for both Ricky and his family was overwhelming. I marveled watching God's creative genius in Rickey's life journey. Ricky overcoming his life challenges is but a tiny indicator of the reward awaiting our trust in God. He will be there for every step as we navigate the rocky roads of life.

Someday, when rounding third and headed for home, we will all hit the end of the trail and most likely be speechless as we step into the presence of our Lord and Savior. I often imagine family and friends who have run the bases ahead of me cheering and rejoicing at my arrival as I slide headfirst into Home...

Life's journey is not easy. Never will be. One of the big mistakes we often make is making it seem like all troubles are over when you embrace Christianity. Unfortunately, that is not in the contract. We will still have problems and heartaches and even tragedies. But we all can have a hope on that rocky road that is sustaining and powerful. Someday we will get to that beautiful destination. Ricky Hill, and his determination to reach his goal, with God's help along the way, was just a teaser for what that magnificent moment could look like in our future.

Rickey's story is very powerful. Not only does the movie communicate an inspiring message about overcoming obstacles, but it also demonstrates what it looks like to keep your faith despite any discouragements you may face along the way. I have often found that to be true in my life and it brings to mind a thought I cherished during my cancer treatments as I recovered from the side effects.

> *"Start by doing what's necessary, then do what's possible, and suddenly you are doing the impossible." St Francis of Assisi* [21]

Although James Hill is a Baptist preacher, and his career is a central part of the story, *THE HILL* avoids preaching. Instead, it demonstrates how God's power and faithfulness are more effectively illustrated focusing on Rickey's narrative rather than trying to preach a sermon. And you know what? For me, God's hand is testimony enough.

### *An Encouraging Attitude:*
Rickey's story illustrates for me that the human spirit is one of ability, perseverance, and courage that no disability can steal away! It proves that hard things are put in our way, not to stop us, but to call out our courage and strength.

126

### *A Spiritual Insight:*

*"Trust in the Lord with all your heart; do not depend on your own understanding. Seek his will in all you do, and he will show you which path to take." Proverbs 3:5-6*

### *A Step to Consider:*

"Start by doing what's necessary, then do what's possible, and suddenly you are doing the impossible." St Francis of Assisi

# Reflection 23

# *"An Unspoken Bond..."*

*September 17, 2023*

*"OUR FRIENDSHIP TRANSCENDS TYPICAL SPEECH. THIS FRIENDSHIP IS ESPECIALLY IMPORTANT BECAUSE IT GIVES ME FAITH THAT MY TRUE SELF IS VALUED IN SPITE OF MY UNRULY BODY."*
***Reece Blankenship***

As many of you know, I have been involved with baseball for many years as a player, coach and even as a scout looking for young players interested in pursuing their dream of playing baseball beyond their high school years. I also keep an eye out for those players who have helped impact other young people in a positive way. Always looking for thoughts on positivity and encouragement. Imagine that!

I recently ran across a story by Anthony Castrovince about one of my favorite players, Atlanta Braves' First Baseman Matt Olson. Matt was originally drafted by the Oakland A's and was traded to the Braves a year ago. Matt has had a baseball breakthrough the past couple of years and has become an MVP-caliber player, while a good friend of Matt's from High School, Reece Blankenship, who is on the autism spectrum, also had a communication breakthrough that allowed him to pursue the dreams once locked inside him.

Now, these pals are both using their hands to make an impact; the 29-year-old Matt with that booming bat vying for the MLB home run crown, and the 28-year-old Reece with the letterboard he points to when spelling out his ideas for how to empower, accept and advocate for those on the spectrum.

This heartwarming friendship, which is documented in a new MLB Network feature "Unspoken Bond," is helping to improve the lives of others. When Matt was still with the Oakland A's, he was an early supporter of ReClif, the business and charity Reece founded to help autistic people and their families. And because of the trade that brought Olson to his hometown team last year, he has been able to ramp up that support by organizing a major fundraiser for ReClif and providing Braves tickets for autistic individuals and their families. This good citizenship earned Olson the Braves' 2023 Roberto Clemente Award nomination. "Matt and I have connected on a different plane," Reece writes. "We each see the deeper being."

For the first 19 years and 11 months of his life, Reece could not communicate such a powerful proclamation of friendship … or anything else. He was, as he writes now, "trapped inside a nightmare," fully capable of understanding the world around him, yet unable to transmit his thoughts. At the time, Reece was diagnosed to have the intellectual capabilities of a three-year-old. He needed a lot of attention. With few autism services available at the time and the cost of professional therapists difficult to manage, Reece's mother, Lou, and father, Jeff, would hire local teenagers, often, athletes, to work with Reece and meet his goal of 36 hours of therapy per week.

Because Reece cannot speak or control his movements, he will sometimes make loud noises or bite his own hand when coping with anxiety or excitement. You can imagine how these quirks of his condition would be received by the average high school student unaccustomed to them. From the beginning, though, Reece's family noted how naturally comfortable Matt was around Reece, his classmate.

The students were trained to engage in "play therapy," helping Reece with learning activities, exercise (walking, biking, swimming, shooting baskets, throwing and kicking balls), writing, and coloring. Matt's older brother, Zack, initially did the job. When he graduated, Matt, who had grown up with Reece's older sister, Daron, took over. "It was an eye-opening experience for me," Matt said.

"Watching them interact, especially when a lot of people are around, you would think that Reece isn't even paying attention to Matt," Lou, Reece's mother said. "Then, you will notice that Reece is standing closer to Matt or grabbing his hand or arm. Or Matt will put his arm around Reece's shoulder. As a mom, I can just see the non-verbal energy between them."

The friendship continued after high school. When Matt was a Minor League player with the A's, his season would wrap up just as Reece's siblings were venturing off to college in the fall. So, Matt would serve a brotherly role for him. "I would get Snapchats from [Matt] of him and Reece together," said Daron, Reece's sister. "It was just very pure, very genuine, and it was so nice to know that, while you're away, somebody was still there with my brother, being a good person for him."

Then, in 2014, Reece had a quantum leap in communication that caught everyone in his orbit, including Matt, by surprise. Reece's parents took him to a "spelling to communicate" workshop where autism patients are taught the motor skills to point to letters on a board to spell words. Reece had done quite a bit of practicing via home-based therapy in the weeks leading up to that moment, yet what came out of him in those few days was nothing short of extraordinary.

The breakthrough came early in the workshop. "We're going to talk about astronomy," one of the therapists said to Reece. "Do you know anything about that?" Reece began pointing to letters on the board, spelling out a complete sentence: "I know Copernicus advocated that the Earth revolves around the sun."

Lou and Jeff looked at each other in amazement. Doctors had told them their son had the intellectual equivalent of a toddler. But in that moment, he proved he had so much more to offer. "The joke's on us," said Matt, "because Reece is probably the smartest person in the room."

What has followed, over the last nine years, is an inspiring story about a young man who was finally able to convey his dreams and the big leaguer who helped him pursue them. As Reece began using a letterboard and, subsequently, a keyboard to reveal ideas he had for a treatment and fitness center for people on the spectrum and others who need individualized attention, his parents began to draw up a business plan. The resulting facility is named ReClif, for his first and middle name, Reece Clifton. Since it opened its doors in Peachtree Corners in early 2018, ReClif has served hundreds of clients with therapy options that include personalized exercise classes, therapeutic yoga, spelling-to-communicate coaching, specialized learning seminars and other offerings.

To launch the business, Reece had solicited support on GoFundMe in 2017. The first donation was a $5,000 submission from his friend Matt, then a rookie with the A's. Matt, his brother and some of their friends also helped move equipment and furniture into the facility when ReClif signed its first lease. "It's a very easy decision," Olson started, "to give back to somebody that I care greatly about, for a cause that I care greatly about and a family that I trust is here to do the right thing for other people."

When Matt was traded to the Braves and signed a long-term extension with them prior to the 2022 season, no one was happier than Reece. Not only could he connect with his friend more frequently, but Matt's platform with the local MLB team has given ReClif additional exposure. Reece has long been amazed at what Matt's hands can do with a baseball and a bat. But now, with the help of his letterboard, his family and his longtime friend Matt, Reece has proven his own hands are pretty powerful, too.

Reece typed out the following on his Letterboard to share his thoughts on his friendship with Matt over all these years... It literally says it all!

Reece writes:

"OUR FRIENDSHIP TRANSCENDS TYPICAL SPEECH. THIS FRIENDSHIP IS ESPECIALLY IMPORTANT BECAUSE IT GIVES ME FAITH THAT MY TRUE SELF IS VALUED IN SPITE OF MY UNRULY BODY.

FIRST OFF FOR ME, MATT IS A GOOD FRIEND BECAUSE HIS UNWAVERING ABILITY FOR CALMNESS IS THE PERFECT FOIL FOR MY UNPREDICTABLE SELF. HE IS WITTY AND INTELLIGENT. HIS WIFE NICOLE IS OF THE SAME ILK AND THEY MAKE A GREAT DUO.

MATT IS SELF ASSURED WITHOUT BEING COCKY AND I SO MUCH ADMIRE HIS ATHLETIC PROWESS. WHILE GROWING UP IT NEVER HURT TO HAVE FRIENDS LIKE MATT WHO WERE BIG, STRONG, AND WELL RESPECTED IN OUR SCHOOL. THIS STILL HOLDS TRUE IN THE REAL WORLD TODAY.

MATT BELIEVES IN ME AND HAS CONSISTENTLY SUPPORTED MY VISION FOR BOTH RECLIF AND RECLIF COMMUNITY. MONETARY CONTRIBUTIONS ASIDE I THINK HIS LOYALTY TO ME, RECLIF AND RECLIF COMMUNITY CERTAINLY MAKES OTHERS AT LEAST TAKE NOTICE AND POSSIBLY INQUIRE DEEPER THAN THEY MIGHT HAVE.

YOU MAY KNOW THAT I HAVE ALWAYS DONE PRESEASON STATS FOR MATT AND FOR MOST YEARS I HAVE BEEN DANG CLOSE. THIS YEAR MATT IS SURPASSING EVEN MY

HIGH PREDICTIONS. SINCE HE HAS ALREADY CRUSHED THE 42 HRS I PREDICTED I ALREADY GAVE HIM PERMISSION TO MAKE MY GUESSES LOOK FOOLISH. LIKE I RECENTLY WROTE TO MATT—SOMETIMES CHEMISTRY MAKES STATISTICAL ANALYSIS GO AWRY. SO, SWING AWAY WITH HAPPY HEARTS AND ENJOY THE STRONG VIBE THIS TEAM IS CREATING."[22]

The heart-touching story of Matt and Reece brings to mind a parable related by Jesus which I think is desperately needed today. I simply can't remember a more contentious cultural climate in my lifetime. As a Christian, I'm often wondering how I can make a difference in an such an environment as we so often see in today's culture. I think modeling the story below related by Jesus in the parable of the Good Samaritan is desperately needed today.

The parable of the Good Samaritan that Jesus told in Luke 10:29-37 is a vital story for everyone to hear and model in our contentious society today. In the parable, Jesus describes a man going from Jerusalem to Jericho who is attacked by robbers who strip him and beat him. A priest and a Levite pass by without helping him, but a Samaritan stops and cares for him, taking him to an inn where the Samaritan pays for his care.

Jesus showed we need to show kindness and compassion to not only the neighbors we are comfortable with, but especially to those we are uncomfortable with. We cannot look away when we encounter any person in need no matter what their color, status, beliefs, disabilities, or behaviors might be. We are called to compassion, and only that kind of faith will cause change.

Matt Olson has modeled this parable so practically in real life from his early high school days all the way through his climb to the status as a candidate for the Most Valuable Player Award this season in Major League Baseball. His take on helping others, especially Reece, will always be in my heart. Matt has made this his simple but profound approach to loving your neighbor, certainly something we can all learn from!

> *"If I can help someone, I don't need to think or pray about it. I just do it."*

That is exactly what Jesus was saying to the religious "expert" who interrogated Him about this parable. Don't rationalize why you can't help your neighbor. If you can help, then you do it. That is how Christianity got an early foothold in an antagonistic culture.

Professor E. Glenn Hinson writes, "The early Christians impressed their culture with high moral standards and their practice of charity for all, regardless of social status."[23] That is the kind of faith that makes a difference. Over two-thousand years later, we still describe those who go above and beyond as 'Good Samaritans'. We need God to help raise up an army of those selfless servants to impact our current culture. Volunteers are needed today. Let's model that practice every chance we get and become that Army of Volunteers!

### *An Encouraging Attitude:*
*"OUR FRIENDSHIP TRANSCENDS TYPICAL SPEECH. THIS FRIENDSHIP IS ESPECIALLY IMPORTANT BECAUSE IT GIVES ME FAITH THAT MY TRUE SELF IS VALUED IN SPITE OF MY UNRULY BODY." Reece Blankenship*

### *A Spiritual Insight:*
*Jesus showed we need to show kindness and compassion to not only the neighbors we are comfortable with, but especially to those we are uncomfortable with. We cannot look away when we encounter any person in need no matter what their color, status, beliefs, disabilities, or behaviors might be. We are called*

*to compassion, and only that kind of faith will cause change.*
*Luke 10:29-37*

### *A Step to Consider:*
"If I can help someone, I don't need to think or pray about it. I just do it." Matt Olson

# Reflection 24

# *"Heaven has Gained Another Angel!"*

*October 13, 2023*

*"When we visited in the Emergency Room, mom held my hand and told me I was her Angel, now, as she joins dad in Heaven, she is my Angel..."*

Mom joined Dad in heaven today… She passed peacefully in her sleep and now joins Dad and all who preceded her in death in their Eternal Home with our Lord in Heaven. It's been a difficult journey for both of us over the past few years given the virus and the isolation it created for so many. Despite her passing, my relationship with mom will continue each and every day for the rest of my life. I will continue to value the lessons she taught me about hard work and caring for others. Those lessons will continue to live on for all our family.

Oh, the memories... The good memories from growing up on the farm, the tastes and smells of the meals she loved to prepare for family and friends, her undying loyalty following both my playing and coaching days and always being there as a listening ear when needed as I faced the ups and downs of a cancer journey. We shared laughs, cries, and all different types of emotions, but the memory I will be forever grateful for occurred when she was rushed to the Medical ICU during COVID; it was a time when her heart rate was sky high, and her blood pressure was dangerously low. My heart was beating out of my chest as I followed the ambulance to the hospital.

I grabbed her hand once we got in the ER, something that wasn't able to happen for many months due to COVID. I told her, "I love you so very much!" She looked at me, squeezed my hand and she didn't have to say a word, I knew how much she loved me. She then added in her own special way... "Heck of a way to get to hold your hand!" Mom then said, "You have always been my Angel." And now, as she joins Dad in Heaven, she is my Angel! Most people can only dream about seeing an angel. I had the pleasure of living my whole life with one and will be remembering her after she flew away into the heavens to be once again united with Dad and other loved ones.

In that moment I realized that I have been on the receiving end of more love from her than most receive in a lifetime. I had no more troubling thoughts about her death at that point. My mom was at peace, and one day I will know that peace too. One day we'll all be in our heavenly home, together again with Mom, who gave my earthly home such meaning. As I grieve her death yet celebrate a life well lived, I find comfort in the following passage from Proverbs which I think describes Mom pretty well...

*"Who can find a virtuous and capable wife? She is worth more than precious rubies. Her husband can trust her, and she will greatly enrich his life. She will not hinder him but help him all her life. She finds wool and flax and busily spins it. She is like a merchant's ship; she brings her food from afar. She gets up before dawn to prepare breakfast for her household and plan the day's work for her servant girls.*

*She goes out to inspect a field and buys it; with her earnings she plants a vineyard. She is energetic and strong, a hard worker. She watches for bargains; her lights burn late into the night. Her hands are busy spinning thread, her fingers twisting fiber. She extends a helping hand to the poor and opens her arms to the needy. She has no fear of winter for her household because all of them have warm clothes.*

*She quilts her own bedspreads. She dresses like royalty in gowns of finest cloth. Her husband is well known, for he sits in the council meeting with the other civic leaders. She makes belted linen garments and sashes to sell to the merchants. She is clothed with strength and dignity, and she laughs with no fear of the future. When she speaks, her words are wise, and kindness is the rule when she gives instructions.*

*She carefully watches all that goes on in her household and does not have to bear the*

141

*consequences of laziness. Her children stand and bless her. Her husband praises her: "There are many virtuous and capable women in the world, but you surpass them all!" Charm is deceptive, and beauty does not last; but a woman who fears the LORD will be greatly praised"* (Proverbs 31: 10-30).

I've realized over time that every time it rains, it stops raining. Every time you hurt; you heal. After darkness always comes light and I will be reminded of this each and every time my special memories of Mom fill my heart and my mind. She will always be a part of who I am. I know this is not the end. She is now free, and at peace. She isn't bound by the confines of her earthly body and is free to laugh, move, dance, and play in ways she hasn't been able to in years. She is now reunited with dad and spending her days with the Lord. She is Home. Mom, please send some comfort and love down to us, especially during these next few weeks...

### *An Encouraging Attitude:*
I've realized over time that every time it rains, it stops raining. Every time you hurt; you heal. After darkness always comes light and I will be reminded of this each and every time my special memories of mom fill my heart and my mind. She will always be a part of who I am.

### *A Spiritual Insight:*
*"Charm is deceptive, and beauty does not last; but a woman who fears the LORD will be greatly praised." Proverbs 31:30*

### *A Step to Consider:*
In that moment I realized that I have been on the receiving end of more love from her than most receive in a lifetime. I had no more troubling thoughts about her death at that point. My mom was at peace, and one day I will know that peace too. One day we'll all be in our heavenly home, together again with Mom, who gave my earthly home such meaning.

# Reflection 25

# *"Finding Hope and Restoration..."*

*November 5, 2023*

*"I've experienced a lot of great things. I've experienced championships. I've experienced hitting big home runs. But seeing the light — coming to Christ — it is the greatest gift I've ever received in my life."*

**Darryl Strawberry**

I had the opportunity to ride along with Darryl Strawberry and Jim Mudd Jr. of Mudd Advertising last Thursday as we traveled to the Juvenile Correction Facility in Eldora where Darryl presented an inspirational message to the young men currently living there. His message was a simple, yet powerful one...

"God has patience with us... He will always love us. His love and Grace will set us free, and the Bible is a simple book that helps provide guidance for our complicated lives."

Darryl shared that his visit to Eldora was about providing hope, explaining that everyone has personal struggles, but some play out more than others...They're suffering from loneliness, brokenness, and we don't always know what happens to them. But I do know one thing – that God loves them regardless of what they're going through – and hopefully the message I brought to them will settle into them so that they can know inside themselves that they can be well, and that's really what it's all about."

Darryl also shared a three-step process that we can all apply in our lives to help us be successful: He describes it with the acronym F.A.T.

Be **F**aithful
Be **A**ccountable
Be **T**eachable

Three simple reminders that we can all apply daily to help us on our life journeys.

Jim Jr. also asked me to introduce Darryl at a Friday morning event in the Mudd Studios and I'm so glad he did! Darryl's message was about the impact the Gospel has had on his life and it was very powerful as he spoke to the overflow crowd in the Studio. I'd encourage you to take some time to listen to Darryl's story and message which Mudd Advertising was kind enough to record so it could be shared. Simply click on the link below to hear Darryl's message of hope and encouragement. You will be glad you did!

https://vimeo.com/880981451/de288ad416?share=copy

Darryl and I do share several things in common... Certainly, we share a love of baseball, but we also share the persistence and patience needed to survive a cancer journey as well as other life challenges that may have come our way, and last but certainly not least, we share our mutual love of our Lord and Savior Jesus Christ.

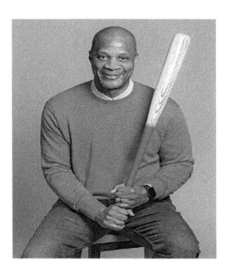

Darryl was perhaps one of the most electrifying players in Major League Baseball history. He entered the league with the New York Mets in 1983. Throughout his 17-year career, he made eight consecutive all-star game appearances and captured four World Series championships. But his baseball prowess on the field at times was largely overshadowed by his controversial lifestyle off of it. It had a lot to do with how and where he grew up. His story is one of both success and failure, a story of perseverance that has led him to become the person he is today.

Darryl is currently working closely with the Mets organization and together with his wife Tracy, they founded the Darryl Strawberry Foundation which is dedicated to children and adults with autism. You can find out more about it at the following link:

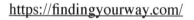

https://findingyourway.com/

For years, Darryl's life was surrounded by controversy, but these days he is a changed man. As Darryl says... "I want people to see the remarkable man I always knew I had the capabilities of being. Not the playing baseball part, but the remarkable man God has shaped me into. I am so proud of what the Lord has done for me and through me..."

With four World Series titles, Darryl is described as a legend by many who have been dazzled by the dynamics of his game. Though Darryl was extremely successful in his career, his personal life was plagued with addiction, abuse, divorce, cancer, and jail time among other issues. Darryl finally found true redemption and restoration in Jesus Christ.

Today, Darryl's purpose and passion is serving the Lord Jesus Christ and helping others transform their lives through the power of the gospel. Darryl travels the country speaking and bringing a message of hope and restoration in Christ.

Darryl shared he likes to use the Book of John to illustrate how he has found hope and restoration from the many challenges he faced as a famous and successful ballplayer. Jesus said to His disciples...

> *"I no longer call you slaves because a master doesn't confide in his slaves. Now you are my friends, since I have told you everything the Father told me"* (John 15:15 NLT).

When we put our faith in Jesus Christ, we begin a special friendship with God. God has given us a user's manual in life called the Bible, which helps us to understand the will of God. God is essentially saying, "Give Me your life, and I will show you My will." The condition of an enlightened mind is a surrendered heart...

God has a plan and a purpose for each of us, but to know the will of God, we must surrender our hearts to Him. Darryl is living proof that by surrendering our heart to God, we can turn away from the things that are troublesome in our lives and enjoy the freedom that God offers each of us as we travel our life's journey with Him.

Many thanks to Jim Jr. and his team for bringing Darryl to the Cedar Valley!

### An Encouraging Attitude:
God has a plan and a purpose for each of us, but to know the will of God, we must surrender our hearts to Him.

### A Spiritual Insight:
*"I no longer call you slaves because a master doesn't confide in his slaves. Now you are my friends, since I have told you every-thing the Father told me" (John 15:15 NLT).*

### A Step to Consider:
When we put our faith in Jesus Christ, we begin a special friendship with God. God has given us a user's manual in life called the Bible, which helps us to understand the will of God. God is essentially saying, "Give Me your life, and I will show you My will." The condition of an enlightened mind is a sur-rendered heart...

# Reflection 26

# *"Showing Love Through Our Actions!"*

*November 24, 2023*

*Liam Doxsee, 9, stands with Iowa baseball athletes during a baseball game at Duane Banks Field in Iowa City this past September. Liam became a part of the Iowa baseball team as its kid captain about a year ago, allowing him access to his favorite sport and team on a deeper and more personal level.*

I felt like writing today after a recent follow-up visit to University Hospitals in Iowa City. It has been a road well-traveled for me, but it seems each time I visit for my checkups, I find something there that inspires me to keep a positive outlook while moving forward on my life journey. Most often, that inspiration comes from walking through the Stead Family Children's Hospital to read the stories of the young patients being treated there. It sits adjacent to the Holden Cancer Center, so it is an easy motivational stop for me.

Most everyone has heard of the halftime "wave" to the kids at the Stead Family Children's Hospital at the U of I football games... It always brings a tear to my eye and a warm feeling in my heart. But are you aware that the University of Iowa baseball team and my good friend Iowa baseball Coach Rick Heller help recognize and support kids in need through the U of I baseball team?

One such young man, Liam Doxsee, recently came to my attention during that recent visit to Iowa City. Liam, who lives in Coal Valley, Illinois, was diagnosed with severe combined immunodeficiency — a rare genetic disorder that affects the immune system — when he was just five days old. About one in 58,000 children are born with SCID each year in the U.S. It is not only a rare disease, but also one that causes pain as well as many other challenges. However, as Liam's mother Mary Matheson often shares: "SCID won't stop this kid." Liam truly lives by this mantra!

At two-months-old, Liam received a bone marrow transplant that saved his life at the Ann & Robert H. Lurie Children's Hospital of Chicago. Now, he visits the University of Iowa Stead Family Children's Hospital a few times every month, takes a variety of medications each morning, afternoon, and night, and gets his nutrients from a gastrostomy tube three times a day.

In a life full of many ups and downs, Liam finds support through family members, friends, and the families three dogs. Liam has quite a HOME TEAM of his own! Matheson said their family works hard to figure out what's best for Liam, deciding who goes with him when he's admitted into the hospital and who stays back to take the other kids to school. "How we support him is just giving him a little bit of grace and time," Matheson said. "…With him and all he's been through; he has a lot of trauma and anxiety." [24]

Liam also leans on Iowa baseball for friendships and support, a relatively new bond he has formed in his young life. As the fourth grader walked down the hallway of Bicentennial Elementary School in Coal Valley, Illinois, in mid-September, one of the teachers asked a few students what their favorite NFL team was. The teacher asked, "What's yours, Liam?" Liam answered quietly, "The Hawks."

A little over a year ago, Liam joined the Iowa baseball team as its Kid Captain, with help from the organization Team IMPACT. This gave Liam the chance to deepen his connections with his favorite team and sport. Between attending a few baseball practices and most games and joining in on pregame huddles, Matheson said Liam treats this opportunity as a job, enjoying every second of it. Liam sat on a bench in the dugout, rolling around a baseball wet from the rain. After the athletes warmed up, they made their way through the dugout, high-fiving and eagerly exchanging "hellos" with Liam. "These are real friendships he's made with the team, which is really special for him," [25] Matheson said.

Liam hugs Iowa head baseball coach Rick Heller before a baseball game at Duane Banks Field in Iowa City.

According to Hawkeye player Ben Wilmes, "Liam is a very loving child and very happy and really doesn't take anything for granted," Wilmes said. "...We see his happiness side because whenever we're together, we take away the aspect of his life in the hospital and kind of help him completely forget about that in the moment." [26]

Not every aspect of Liam's life involves new experiences. Liam said living with SCID is a challenge, especially having to go to doctor appointments often as a kid with a sensitive body. "Especially the needles," Liam said. "See, the longer needles, everyone says they don't hurt a lot. But when I feel them, it's like I'm getting thrown into a firepit. It hurts bad." [27]

After a long day at the hospital, Liam and his mom usually walk over to a cafe at the University of Iowa Stead Family Children's Hospital and order him a vanilla steamer. Along with the challenges Liam encounters, Matheson said the family deals with financial hardships that come with multiple doctor appointments and frequent travel from their home in Coal Valley to Iowa City, which takes over an hour.

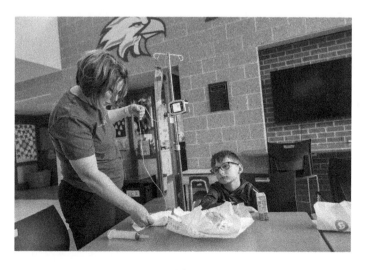

Despite occasional overwhelming hardships, Matheson said she's grateful for the family's switch to the University of Iowa Stead Family Children's Hospital, as it improved Liam's health and introduced him to new experiences in Iowa. "The move did a lot for Liam," Matheson said, "it also partnered us with…everybody in Iowa too."

Personally, I am so very grateful not only to the Hawkeye baseball squad for their caring love and support of Liam and other Kid Captains they host at Duane Banks Field, but I'm also very thankful for facilities such as the Ronald McDonald House and Hope Lodge that sit adjacent to the ballpark that help defray the costs of travel and treatments.

Hope Lodge provided me and my family so much support, from not only providing a room to call home during treatments, but also providing a kitchen where I could prepare meals, seek support group help, enjoy exercise opportunities, participate in music therapy to help me sleep and deal with the pain of treatments, but most importantly, to interact with a group of fellow cancer patients who I built trusting and caring relationships with as we discussed tips, assistance, advice, and guidance on our situations… but most importantly, how to deal with the unknowns of the treatments that lay ahead…

This story reminds me that Jesus is our role model—when we serve others sacrificially, we show love the way He did. Pop songs, movies, and books shape the way we think about love. Attraction, emotion, romance, and sentiment color how we expect it to be. But when the Lord told His followers that they're to love the way He does, He wasn't talking about what we find in popular culture. Jesus gave them the ultimate image of self-sacrificing love: a person laying down his life for a friend (John 15:13).

The kind Jesus was referring to looks far more like the sacrificial service of a caregiver changing a soiled adult diaper. It looks like a family opening their home to foster children. Or like a baseball team finding time to make a young person

155

feel wanted and special while facing challenging health issues. Sacrificial love is humbly given by countless modern heroes of the faith every day as they lay down their hopes and dreams to meet the needs of the sick, helpless, and broken among us.

And we should remember that when Jesus spoke the words in the passage above, He was just hours away from laying down His innocent life for each one of us—those He loves.

As the following verse in Philippians shares, "Let each of you look not only to his own interests, but also to the interests of others (Philippians 2:4).

I firmly believe that Christians should always look for ways to show love through our actions. Our thoughts and prayers need hands and feet displaying the love of Christ to have eternal impact. It is hard to spend much time in the New Testament and not realize the challenge for Christians toward those hurting, in need, and devoid of hope. I know that I am challenging myself to be willing to be the hands and feet that reflect the love of Christ. May each of us feel free to focus on the One who has given us hope in this challenging season to be a light in the darkness that surrounds us.

### *An Encouraging Attitude:*
When the Lord told His followers that they're to love the way He does, He wasn't talking about what we find in popular culture. Jesus gave them the ultimate image of self-sacrificing love: a person laying down his life for a friend (John 15:13).

### *A Spiritual Insight:*
*"Let each of you look not only to his own interests, but also to the interests of others (Philippians 2:4).*

### *A Step to Consider:*
Christians should be looking for ways to show love through our actions. Our thoughts and prayers need hands and feet displaying the love of Christ to have eternal impact. It is hard to

spend much time in the New Testament and not realize the challenge for Christians toward those hurting, in need, and devoid of hope.

# Reflection 27

# *"Finding Hope in Hurt..."*

*December 18, 2023*

*We can all find Hope in the Hurt! Whatever hardships we may be walking through, we must have hope and trust that God is painting a picture of wholeness and transformation, even if we can't see it, we need to look for beauty and goodness—it is there. I am trusting that promise for myself and my friends and family who may be hurting...*

I'm just returning from an appointment in Iowa City and wanted to take some time to reflect a bit... Prior to my appointment, I had the opportunity to visit with several friends who have been hurting, both physically and emotionally. Being in community with others often means we share joys, sorrows, and yes, even hurts. Sometimes the sorrows and hurts come in waves and all you can do is care, pray, and be present.

Even good people often deal with sorrow and hurt, it's all around us and it is easy to lose heart. The daily news stories we hear in the media typically tend to focus on tragedy and heartbreaking sadness... and it can literally wear a person out! Been there, done that!

On the drive home from my appointment today, I got to thinking that life doesn't always send us a recipe filled with tasty entrees, but often there are some bitter ingredients that may accompany whatever is being "dished out" to us in life.

I've learned a few things about preparing food the past few years and I've learned that often, those "bitter" ingredients can be combined to make a delicious entrée. Those ingredients certainly may not taste good on their own, actually, some can taste pretty nasty on their own... ever taste pure flour, baking soda, raw eggs or avocado oil on their own? No thanks!

I do think, however, that God sends us bitter ingredients at times in our lives for a purpose. After all, Paul says in the Book of Romans:

> *"We know that God causes everything to work together for the good of those who love God and are called according to his purpose for them"*
> *(Romans 8:28).*

Notice that verse does not say that everything in our lives is going to be good... Just take a quick look at today's news headlines which certainly proves that isn't true! And it doesn't say this promise is for everyone—just those who love God. The way God works all things together for good is kind of like preparing a good meal, let's just say to fit this time of year, a Christmas meal!

WHEN HOPE HURTS

In our lives and in the world, there will be elements that are bitter and unpleasant. I know I've often thought after preparing one of my meals, "That doesn't taste very good..." imagine that! Or after I've had to make some adjustments in my life, "I don't like that change in my life." Or after listening to the news, "I don't like what's happening in the world today."

When I'm in a season of change, and some of those elements that come my way don't "taste" very good, I try my best not to become bitter by seeing only the negative in my circumstances. Because even when I can't see it, I trust that God takes it all—the good and the bitter—and uses it for His good plan in my life. I may not see it now, but I hope to taste its "sweetness" in Heaven one day.

I always like to listen to some music on the drive home from my appointments which is comforting as I ponder test results, diagnoses, and medical plans moving forward as a cancer survivor. A song I heard today really found a place in my heart as its lyrics spoke to me about finding some hope in the hurt that has come not only my way on this cancer journey, but also the hurt being experienced by some of my friends...

The lyrics asked the question that we all tend to struggle with... That question being: why?

The song's title was "The Hurt and the Healer" by Mercy Me.[28]

Here are a few of the verses from the song that stuck with me today.

Why?
The question that is never far away,
The healing doesn't come from the explained,
Jesus please don't let this go in vain.
You're all I have,
All that remains.
So here I am,
What's left of me,
Where glory meets my suffering.
I'm alive!

Even though a part of me has died
You take my heart and breathe it back to life.
I'll fall into Your arms open wide...
When the hurt and the healer collide.

Sometimes I feel it's all that I can do.
Pain so deep that I can hardly move.
Just keep my eyes completely fixed on You,
Lord take hold and pull me through!

Jesus come and break my fear,
Awake my heart and take my tears
Find Your glory even here,
When the hurt and the healer collide...

I surely can't explain why things happen in life... Sometimes, I guess it is simply life weighing in. I have learned over the years however that Jesus does not let suffering go in vain. I have witnessed over and over how God redeems sadness and tragedy. He so often brings beauty out of ashes... When we struggle to see how any good can come out of a trial either ourselves or that others may be facing, we need to place our trust and faith in our Lord and Savior. We won't necessarily "feel" that, but we can move forward with the understanding that God will never let us down, and that He never will!

> *"Dear friends, don't be surprised at the fiery trials you are going through, as if something strange were happening to you. Instead, be very glad—for these trials make you partners with Christ in his suffering, so that you will have the wonderful joy of seeing his glory when it is revealed to all the world" (1 Peter 4: 12-13).*

Count me among those who tried to dance around this truth for as long as I could. Be very glad? Seriously? But when you have nowhere else to turn but to Christ you find out that you should have turned to Him first all along! Jesus knows the human condition. He has already been where we are. When the hurt and the Healer collide something amazing happens. The pain may not immediately go away, but peace and hope begin to slowly heal the pain.

> *"In his kindness God called you to share in his eternal glory by means of Christ Jesus. So, after you have suffered a little while, He will restore, support, and strengthen you, and He will place you on a firm foundation" (1 Peter 5: 10).*

That is a promise that we can hold on to in times of sorrow and suffering. We can all find Hope in the Hurt! Whatever hardships we may be walking through, we must have hope and trust that God is painting a picture of wholeness and transformation, even if we can't see it, we need to look for beauty and goodness—it is there, and I am trusting that promise for myself and my friends and family who may be hurting.

### *An Encouraging Attitude:*
We can all find Hope in the Hurt! Whatever hardships we may be walking through, we must have hope and trust that God is painting a picture of wholeness and transformation, even if we can't see it, we need to look for beauty and goodness—it is there. I am trusting that promise for myself and my friends and family who may be hurting...

### *A Spiritual Insight:*
*"In his kindness God called you to share in his eternal glory by means of Christ Jesus. So, after you have suffered a little while, He will restore, support, and strengthen you, and He will place you on a firm foundation" (1 Peter 5: 10).*

### *A Step to Consider:*
When you have nowhere else to turn but to Christ you find out that you should have turned to Him first all along! Jesus knows the human condition. He has already been where we are. When the hurt and the Healer collide something amazing happens. The pain may not immediately go away, but peace and hope begin to slowly heal the pain.

# Reflection 28

# *"Where God's Love is, there is no Fear..."*

### *January 1, 2024*

*As we step into 2024, let's remember that by being forgiving, being kind, staying honest, finding joy, doing good and giving our best, we not only elevate ourselves, but empower those around us to learn more, do more and become who they were meant to be...*

As we enter a New Year, I've reflected on 2023. One lesson I've learned and tried to take to heart is that many of life's challenges can so often make us nervous, instilling a bit of fear and anxiety in our souls. During those moments, I've also learned to take a pause and focus on how much those in our lives love us, knowing that they are on our side, wanting us to succeed, while supporting us with their strength and love. Certainly, my definition of a "Home Team". I've been blessed in that regard and offer my heartfelt thanks to those on my "Home Team"!

As we look around us in today's world, there may be ample reason to feel fear, but it seems to me that love moves against fear. When love comes in the front door of our hearts, fear tends to go out the back door. We can't be afraid and loving at the same time—not with real love. When we have real love— God's love, and the love of those supporting us on our life journey — then we don't have to fear.

Scripture points out:

"Where God's love is, there is no fear, because God's perfect love drives out fear" (1 John 4:18 NCV).

God doesn't want us to fail. He wants us to succeed at what we may be doing while fulfilling our purpose. When we focus on His love, we have no reason to be afraid because perfect love casts out all fear! The more loving we are, the less fearful we are. So, if we make love the motivation for what we do, we are not going to be afraid to do it.

I think back to 2023 and many of the examples where love overcame fear. First responders running into a burning building to rescue children because of love, putting aside their own personal safety. Parents putting their own lives at risk to protect their families because they love their children. If love is the motivation of everything we do, then fear is going to disappear. Just a couple good examples of how to face the challenges and burdens that life can often "pitch" our way!

Simply put... Make love your motivation to help eliminate the fear and anxiety that life challenges can bring on.

As I was doing some reading this morning, standing at the threshold of a New Year, I came across a passage from Mother Teresa that really touched my heart and provided some guidance for me in 2024. May we all draw some inspiration and guidance from her as we embark on next steps on our life journey in 2024...

Mother Teresa writes:

- People are often unreasonable and self-centered.

  Forgive them anyway.

- If you are kind, people may accuse you of ulterior motives.

  Be kind anyway.

- If you are honest, people may cheat you.

  Be honest anyway.

- If you find happiness, people may be jealous.

  Be happy anyway.

- The good you do today may be forgotten tomorrow.

  Do good anyway.

- Give the world the best you have, and it may never be enough.

  Give your best anyway. [29]

As we move forward into 2024, let's carry Mother Teresa's timeless wisdom as a torch lighting our path. In forgiving, being kind, staying honest, finding joy, doing good and giving our best, we not only elevate ourselves but empower those around us to learn more, do more and become who they were meant to be.

May 2024 be a year of meaningful growth filled with the same love for each other that God has for each of us!

### *An Encouraging Attitude:*
Simply put... Make love your motivation to help eliminate the fear and anxiety that life challenges can bring on.

### *A Spiritual Insight:*
*"Where God's love is, there is no fear, because God's perfect love drives out fear."* 1 John 4:18 (NCV)

### *A Step to Consider:*
As we move forward into 2024, let's carry Mother Teresa's timeless wisdom as a torch lighting our path. In forgiving, being kind, staying honest, finding joy, doing good and giving our best, we not only elevate ourselves but empower those around us to learn more, do more and become who they were meant to be.

# Reflection 29

# *"Conversation with a Complete Stranger"*

*January 15, 2024*

*I'm so very thankful for the conversation I was blessed to have with a complete stranger at Mayo Clinic about "Nearing Home". May the world be blessed with many similar conversations...*

J ust home from a "tune up" at Mayo Clinic this past week to help correct some ongoing issues. I'm so very thankful to be blessed with great medical teams at both Mayo Clinic and the University of Iowa Hospitals. Some adjustments made, and as I always say, 'Life is about adjustments..."

As is often the case, I have the opportunity to visit with others while in the waiting rooms at both of these institutions, many of whom are experiencing challenges similar and often far worse than what I have been through. This past week's visit offered that opportunity, and triggered some reflection which has been good for me, and hopefuly you.

While waiting for my final consult after doing a number of labs, I was seated by a gentleman, a bit older than me who was there for a similar follow up. He shared he was a three time cancer survivor and was a retired teacher and coach from the inner city Chicago area... Imagine that, and what a conversation that developed into! He shared he was of Puero Rican descent and coached high school baseball and basketball there.

Of course the first question I asked was who his favorite baseball player was guessing we may have a similar player in mind And yes, we both shared an admiration for a similar player by the name of Roberto Clemente, who was a Puerto Rican native. One thing led to another, and we discussed Roberto and the fact that sadly, his brilliant Major League career was cut short by a tragic accident in 1972.

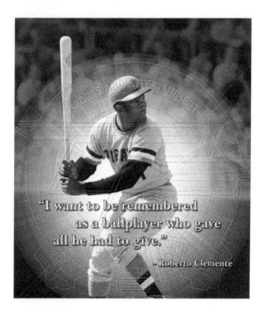

"I want to be remembered as a ballplayer who gave all he had to give."

– Roberto Clemente

On Dec. 31, 1972 Puerto Rican <u>Roberto Clemente</u> died in a plane crash while traveling at great risk in response to urgent requests to deliver help to earthquake devastated Nicaragua. I was a senior in high school at that time with baseball in full swing. We both agreed that his tragic death had a tremendous impact in both our lives, not just because he was killed, but instead, because of the purpose he was pursuing when his plane crashed.

Roberto Clemente had many friends in Nicaragua. He was also haunted by the thoughts of the children he had visited there over the years. In twenty-four hours' time he had set up the Roberto Clemente Committee for Nicaragua. Fear for his friends was supplanted by fury when he heard stories of Nicaragua's Dictator Anastozia Somoza's troops seizing aid for their own enrichment. Clemente decided that he himself would have to go to Nicaragua to make sure the aid got where it was supposed to go.

On December 31, 1972, he boarded a ramshackle plane overloaded with relief supplies . . . The plane went down a thousand yards out to sea and Clemente's body was never recovered . . .

I shared that in my opinion, Roberto Clemente was simply a man, a man who strove to achieve his dream of peace and justice for oppressed people throughout the world, something I will always remember about him. To me, that memory is much more significant than the accolades he received as an outstanding baseball player, although he was certainly that!

Our conversation then went a bit deeper as my new acquaintance shared he had often asked himself the question of how he wanted to be remembered as a teacher/coach as he was "nearing home" on his life journey with cancer. He shared that often, his body felt like the torn and tattered cover of a baseball that had been used and worn out from its "time in the game."

He went on to share that "...After I die, I'd like to be remembered for the work I've done in my life. I know not all my work will be remembered. I doubt anyone will recall many of my efforts, but I do hope some of what I've done as a coach, teacher, mentor, and leader will be worthy of remembrance." He went on, "Plus, let me be clear: an essential part of my life's work has been as a husband, father, son, grandson, brother, and uncle."

I told him that he is not alone in pondering how he may want to be remembered for the work he has done. I've also had similar thoughts on my life journey as I feel it is a common human desire. We should wish to be remembered for our work makes sense considering one of the first things we learn in Scripture is what it means to be human. In Genesis 1, God, who is revealed to us as the "first worker", creates human beings in God's own image. We are made to be workers, right from the start. But, as Genesis 2 makes clear, God created human beings to work in the world, to help the world be productive and to care for it (Gen 2:15). Given the fact of work being a central part our basic nature, it makes sense that we should want to be remembered for the work we have done in life as we fulfill God's created intentions for us.

Now, let me assure you that I don't think either one of us were obsessed with our death or even our individual legacy. But I have at times wondered how I will be remembered after I die because I've been to more and more funerals the past few years given my stage in life. It's something that comes naturally with aging.

On my way home from Mayo Clinic, I had some time to reflect on how I may be remembered after I'm gone... I'm glad this question visited my consciousness. Why? Because the "How will I be remembered after I'm gone?" question leads to other questions, like: "Am I investing my life in the things that matter most? Am I spending the limited time I have on this earth in fulfillment of my life's purpose? Am I nurturing deep, loving relationships with people, especially those who are close to me? Am I living each day in a way that reflects the presence and grace of Christ?"

As followers of Jesus, we are tasked to join our Lord in his redemptive, restorative work. Just as Roberto Clemente was doing when he boarded that plane to help bring aid to his friends in Nicaragua, our work as followers of Jesus includes all that we do to bear witness to him, to make disciples, to seek his kingdom and to love our neighbors. Often, we do this work as members of a church, where we contribute to the growth of the church as the body of Christ (Eph 4:11-16). We share in the church's work of feeding the hungry, embracing the marginalized, and caring for those who are often overlooked by society.

By reflecting on how you'd like to be remembered I'm not trying to motivate you to polish your image, to make yourself look better for the sake of your post-mortem reputation. Rather, I feel the point of thinking about how you'll be remembered is to inspire you to live and work today with greater integrity, faithfulness, love, and purpose. If I want to be remembered as a caring person, then I am reminded to care more actively for the people in my life, including the folks I engage with through my daily work.

After more than five decades after his death, we recently celebrated the life of Martin Luther King Jr. And we didn't celebrate his Nobel Peace Prize, his three or four hundred other awards or where he went to school. We celebrated a man who offered to lay down his life, each day, in striving to be first in love, moral excellence, generosity and equality.

To conclude today's reflection, our awards, trophies, diplomas and job titles will fade. But striving to be first in love, showing up for others, and making our lives about something far bigger than ourselves will be remembered not only after our death, but will positively change the world while we are alive. Let's all strive to be first in that race!

I'm so very thankful for the conversation I was blessed to have with a complete stranger at Mayo Clinic about "Nearing Home". May the world be blessed with many similar conversations.

### An Encouraging Attitude:
Our awards, trophies, diplomas, and job titles will fade. But striving to be first in love, showing up for others, and making our lives about something far bigger than ourselves will be remembered not only after our death, but will positively change the world while we are alive. Let's all strive to be first in that race!

### A Spiritual Insight:
*"God created human beings to work in the world, to help the world be productive and to care for it" (Gen 2:15).*

### A Step to Consider:
As followers of Jesus, we are tasked to join our Lord in his redemptive, restorative work. Just as Roberto Clemente was doing when he boarded that plane to help bring aid to his

friends in Nicaragua, our work as followers of Jesus includes all that we do to bear witness to Him, to make disciples, to seek His kingdom and to love our neighbors.

# Reflection 30

# *"WHOSE WE ARE* and *WHO WE ARE."*

## *February 10, 2024*

*"The honor of my race, family and self are at stake. Everyone is expecting me to do big things. I will!"*
**Jack Trice October 5, 1923**

Well, it is Super Bowl weekend and I'm sure many of us will be watching with excitement as the Kansas City Chiefs and the San Francisco 49ers battle for the crown of being named the 2024 Super Bowl Champion.

Leading up to this Sunday's game, I recall watching the Buffalo Bills and Kansas City Chiefs game in the Divisional playoff series and I know many of us all heard the same, sickening words uttered by Jim Nantz that Al Michaels uttered three decades before regarding the Bills: "Wide right." A field goal that would decide if Buffalo's season would move on ended in disappointment, a single flaw unraveling a chance at victory.

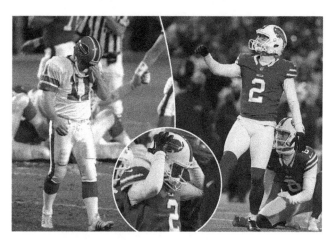

As I sat and watched the CBS telecast of the recent Buffalo-Kansas City playoff game, I thought of how that one statement describes the feelings many of us sometimes have about our lives: that "we're just off." We try to do the things we should when we need to do them; we live a life that is to be respected, admired, maybe even celebrated. Yet, when it comes down to it, a fatal flaw or single mistake can keep us from attaining the triumph we so greatly wish we could experience. If lives end with that feeling of emptiness that comes from falling after coming so close, it could feel utterly devastating...

All of us will go through moments in this life journey where we're off; where we miss just "wide right" on the opportunities in our lives. We can still celebrate knowing we will certainly fall short in our time here; knowing we're going to miss, sometimes even "wide right" at critical moments in our lives. We can celebrate because we know the moments where we miss don't define who we are or the measure of our time on this earth. Instead, we celebrate because we know we are on a collision course with a time where we will be made new, as the apostle Paul wrote in 2 Corinthians 5.

> *"Therefore, if anyone is in Christ, the new creation has come: The old has gone, the new is here!" 2 Corinthians 5:17*

Given the fact February is also Black History Month, I've been enjoying some of my favorite films over the past few weeks that shed light on the struggles for racial inequality in the United States. Much of our history is accurately portrayed, and there are many lessons to be learned in these films!

Some of these movies include:

*42:* The story of baseball legend Jackie Robinson as the first Black player in Major League Baseball.

*Remember the Titans:* The story of the city of Alexandria, Virginia's merging in 1971 of a Black and a White school's Football programs.

*Hidden Figures:* A movie based on the true story of three Black women who were essential to the success of early space flight at NASA.

*Selma:* The story of Martin Luther King and his battle for voting suffrage in the South.

I've also just finished an outstanding book that was gifted to me at Christmas titled *THE IDEALIST.* I highly recommend it!

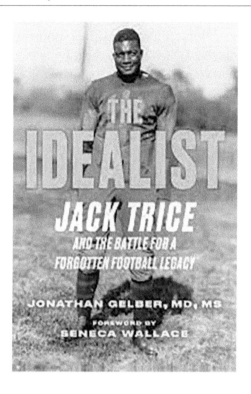

As many of you may know, I am a fan of Iowa State University having coached and earned my master's degree there. Given that, I was never fully aware of Jack Trice's story, an essential story of understated courage, the lasting power of a name, and the battle to honor a pioneering legacy! The book was inspirational and eye opening for me, not only about Jack and his journey, but also about shedding light on the struggles regarding racial inequality in the community of Ames, Iowa, and Iowa State College.

On the eve of his second varsity football game for the Iowa State Cyclones, Jack Trice wrote in a letter, *"The honor of my race, family and self are at stake. Everyone is expecting me to do big things. I will!"* [30]

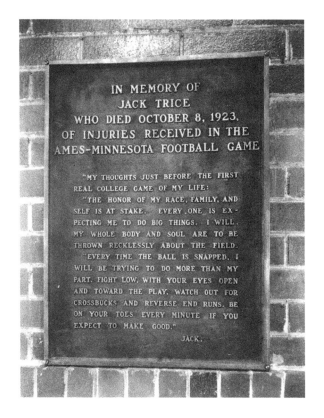

The introspective 21-year-old was very much aware of his status in 1923 as the college's first Black football player. Jack Trice would die tragically days later after sustaining injuries on the field during that game. Today, Iowa State football games are played at Jack Trice Stadium.

***THE IDEALIST*** is a complete portrait of Jack Trice, the son of a former Buffalo Soldier who became a high school football standout in Ohio where he attended the same high school as Olympian Jesse Owens. He embarked on his college career hoping to emulate fellow Iowa State alum George Washington Carver in the field of Agriculture. It is also the story of those who fought for his legacy across generations.

So... what defines a hero? Who has been overlooked because of the color of their skin? In the 1970s, the students of Iowa State asked the same questions. The discovery of the story behind a small, dusty plaque honoring Trice spawned a decades long campus movement to honor a forgotten football hero who helped break racial boundaries and may have died because of them. His faith, perseverance, work ethic and team loyalty were truly inspirational.

As more light is shed on racial inequality in the United States, the story of how Jack Trice's memory led to a namesake stadium—the first and only major football stadium named for an African American individual—should serve an inspiration for all, I know it certainly was for me!

So, when we find ourselves struggling to relate to someone, for whatever reason, or maybe just missing "wide right" at critical moments in our lives, reading and viewing the stories above have reminded me that we are all children of God! As John shares:

> *"Dear friends, let us continue to love one another, for love comes from God. Anyone who loves is a child of God and knows God."* 1 John 4:7

Just maybe we can all pause for a bit this Super Bowl weekend to consider two things: *"WHOSE WE ARE* and *WHO WE ARE."* We are children of God. A God who went to great lengths to love us even though we were unlovable. So, how would a child of God respond victoriously? We show love!

What should encourage all of us, though, is how God is building a time for those who trust in Him and His Son where the snaps, holds and kicks of our lives will be right down the middle. We just have to put our trust in Christ and follow Him with all our hearts. He's promised to take care of the rest after that.

### An Encouraging Attitude:
Just maybe we can all pause for a bit this Super Bowl weekend to consider two things: *"WHOSE WE ARE* and *WHO WE ARE"*. We are children of God. A God who went to great lengths to love us even though we were unlovable. So, how would a child of God respond victoriously? We show love!

### A Spiritual Insight:
*"Dear friends, let us continue to love one another, for love comes from God. Anyone who loves is a child of God and knows God."* 1 John 4:7

### A Step to Consider:
What should encourage all of us, though, is how God is building a time for those who trust in Him and His Son where the snaps, holds and kicks of our lives will be right down the middle. We just have to put our trust in Christ and follow Him with all our hearts. He's promised to take care of the rest after that.

# Reflection 31

# *"Keep me in Your Heart, I'll Stay There Forever"*

*February 25, 2024*

*"If ever a day comes where we can't be together,*
*keep me in your heart, I'll stay there forever"*
*Winnie the Pooh*

This is my favorite time of year. This is when MLB's off-season comes to a close, pitchers and catchers begin to report, and players, coaches, staff, and fans are full of reasonable, radical, and, some might argue, ridiculous hopes and dreams. This is when every team has the same record of 0-0, when things start to warm up, and when we can get our Spring Training on.

You'll see the locker rooms, training facilities, and playing fields, are full of athletes young and old, rookies and veterans, some who will never make the big leagues, others who have had solid careers, and a very select few who will be first ballot hall-of-famers. This time of year is certainly something I will always keep in my heart!

With a new season on the horizon, this is also the time of year that leads me to some reflection over the past year. I'm reaching the age when it becomes a season of losing friends and parents of friends. Certainly, never an easy thing.

Having lost my mother this past fall and attending the visitation of the father of one of my former players this past week, the following tribute to those who have cared for our parents truly touched my heart... It was shared with me by a friend. It reads...

*"For the daughter or son who cared for their parents,*

*This day has extra meaning for you because you've mothered or fathered backwards. But you wouldn't have it any other way.*

*You've driven them to doctors' appointments and made countless phone calls to insurance companies.*

*Like you loaded your kids in and out of your car when they were young, you've done the same for your parents. Making sure they are comfortable, and gently buckling them in.*

*You've cut up meals into tiny bites and held a cup to their tired lips when they've been tired.*

*You've found just the right way to give them their medicine and tried your best to give them a schedule while still giving them independence.*

*You've taken them out for special occasions and taken them for drives just so they can see the Christmas lights one more time.*

*Just like you they dealt with your 15-year-old stubborn attitude, you've worked though their 90-year-old stubbornness and ways.*

*And when they were afraid of dying, you reminded them of how wonderful heaven would be, just like they did when they tucked you in at night when you were a little boy or girl.*

*You take such great care of the things that are important to them; the photos and their prized possessions, making sure their favorite clothes are hung up just right, just like when your mom washed your favorite teddy bear when you spilled juice on it and ironed your new dress on Easter morning. Or when your dad comforted you when you skinned your knee when you were learning to ride your bike or after a heart-breaking loss after a sporting event.*

*And when they called out in the middle of the night because they were afraid they might have fallen out of bed, you came beside them to remind them they were safe. Oh, how many nights they came to your bed and comforted you.*

*You were the first one to drive them to wherever it was when you got that call. Something was wrong, your plans had to change, because your parent needed to be cared for. They needed either their son or daughter.*

*And when the time came to say goodbye, you were right there. Holding their hand, reminding them of just how much they were loved and cherished. You knew they were ready to go, but you weren't. You weren't ready to say goodbye to your mom or dad. You weren't ready to stop mothering or fathering your parent.*

*You couldn't bear to say goodbye to that face, those hands. That body who you loved, that body who cared for you, and who you cared for. The memories you have etched on your soul your entire life, and in these last years the soul you cared for with such mercy and tenderness.*

*Because no matter how much you mothered or fathered your own parent, that person was still your mother or father. And the years you spent loving them, the seasons of frustration and exhaustion... you wouldn't take a second of it back.*

*You have no regrets.*

*No regrets, only peace. Because what better way to say 'I love you' than by mothering or fathering your parents."* [31]

As I've processed my mother's passing, I wanted to share something that I've learned about myself. I've learned I am terrible at accepting praise and help and much more comfortable giving it. I'm think it most likely has something to do with the cancer journey I have experienced. I'm going to change that because it is not very fair to the people in my life.

Devon Bandison used the following analogy when talking about accepting help or compliments. "When someone gives us a compliment or does something for us, it's like they are handing us a wonderful cake that they spent time baking. When we dismiss the compliment or immediately feel like we must do something for them in return for what they just did, it's like we are taking that cake and smashing it back in the other person's face." [32]

We are all taught to be strong, but sometimes the strongest thing we can do is accept help. We are all taught to be modest, but sometimes the best thing we can do when we receive a compliment is simply to say thank you. Give them the gift of the good feeling that comes from helping another person. And in taking my own advice... thank you once again for being part of my Home Team!

As I process the beginning of a new season, both in baseball and in life without my parents, as well as others I have loved throughout my life, I tend to lean on a verse from Proverbs...

*"Let love and faithfulness never leave you; bind them around your neck, write them on the tablet of your heart." Proverbs 3:3*

**An Encouraging Attitude:**
"If ever a day comes where we can't be together, keep me in your heart, I'll stay there forever" Winnie the Pooh

## *A Spiritual Insight:*

*"Let love and faithfulness never leave you; bind them around your neck, write them on the tablet of your heart." Proverbs 3:3*

## *A Step to Consider:*

We are all taught to be strong, but sometimes the strongest thing we can do is accept help. We are all taught to be modest, but sometimes the best thing we can do when we receive a compliment is simply to say thank you. Give them the gift of the good feeling that comes from helping another person.

# Reflection 32

# *"Don't Let the Old Man In!"*

*March 9, 2024*

*The next time I face any anxieties that life may bring my way, I will face them with a positive attitude and won't "LET THE OLD MAN IN!"*

On my recent drive to Dallas, I started pondering why I care so much about the game of baseball…My reasoning boils down to three core elements:

1. I love the game of baseball. My soul is intertwined with it. Hitting, fielding, competing, being part of a team, the smell of fresh cut grass, which brought back so many memories of spring trips south leaving the cold of Iowa behind, and just being on a baseball field feels like home.

2. I love helping people. There's an indescribable joy I feel when witnessing a young player blossom. If you've coached long enough, or scouted long enough, you can probably relate.

3. Baseball is hands down one of the best games for developing essential life skills. I wouldn't be half the person I am today if it weren't for the years of competing and having tough conversations with coaches and players. To this day, my best friends are my baseball friends, garnered over some 60 years in the game.

I often dream of a world where everyone could drink deeply from the well of experiences that baseball offers–to know the joy, the pain, the camaraderie, and the personal growth that comes hand-in-hand with the game!

I also enjoyed my drive south by listening to a song written by Toby Keith which really "hit home" with me given my 60+ years in the game. The song was titled "Don't Let the Old Man In". That song, along with the game of baseball has many incredibly helpful applications in my life as I grow older.

Toby Keith wrote the song after a conversation with Clint Eastwood while they were playing golf. Clint was about to celebrate his 88th birthday by filming a new movie. Toby Keith was blown away and asked him, "how do you do it, man?" Eastwood answered, "I just get up every morning and go out. And I don't let the old man in." [33]

That stuck in Toby Keith's mind, and he penned the song that was featured in the movie "The Mule". The lyrics are inspiring for me in this season of my life.

As the mileage piles up on my life odometer, and the aches and pains make it easy to slow down and quit pushing myself, challenging myself to get out and live life as fully as I can for as long as I can is enormously fulfilling.

> "Many moons I have lived,
> My body's weathered and worn,
> Ask yourself how would you be,
> If you didn't know the day you were born..." [34]

I still have a few moons to catch up to Clint Eastwood, but I need to follow his example. I am still young at heart and my goal is to live out of that feeling for as long as I can, and to try my best to encourage others to do the same. Don't let the old man in helps convince me to live life joyfully and fully and I know that I want to leave it all on life's playing field until I no longer can.

There is another area of life that I must concentrate on, not letting the old man in. This is much more valuable than how I live my life, simply trying to age well. In the Bible Paul talks about how all of us are born with the "old man" or sin nature of Adam. When we decide to follow Jesus, we become a new creation, and a "new man" now resides in us. Simply put, the old man is who I was before I knew Jesus. The "new man" is who I am now that I am a follower of Christ.

Paul talks about the finished work of Jesus on the Cross that gives the new man in us the power to change our frustrating responses when the old man ruled our lives. Jesus conquered the old man and gave us the opportunity to experience a new man within. As Paul shares in Romans...

> *"We know that our old man was crucified with him so that the body of sin would no longer dominate us, so that we would no longer be enslaved to sin" (Romans 6:6 NET)*

The "old man" was crucified, which means the old man is dead. I am a new creation and that new man living in my heart gives me the power to live more like Jesus. Will I live a sinless life? No way. But as I grow in this truth, sin should no longer control me. I have the power within me to deal with sin in a way that will encourage spiritual growth in Christ.

So, this song by Toby Keith takes on a wonderful spiritual meaning for me. I don't want the "old man" to dominate me in my life journey with Jesus. When I battle the fleshly responses that create shame and guilt, I need to remember that the old man is dead. I can set aside those old man impulses. I have the new man living in me through the Holy Spirit and that gives me the freedom to respond differently. The new man lives in my heart, and I need to focus daily on that truth. When I struggle with those impulses, I need to remember the powerful words of this song! Don't let the old man in...

https://m.youtube.com/watch?v=pFfQDqY6mC4

The song has extra personal meaning for me as Toby was battling stomach cancer at the age of 62 while creating and performing the song. He passed on February 5, 2024, after fighting his battle with grace and courage.

To conclude... The next time I face the anxieties that life may bring my way, I will face them with a positive attitude and won't "LET THE OLD MAN IN!"

### *An Encouraging Attitude:*
Clint Eastwood was about to celebrate his 88th birthday by going to film a new movie. Toby Keith was blown away and asked him "how do you do it, man?" Eastwood answered, "I just get up every morning and go out. And I don't let the old man in." [33]

### *A Spiritual Insight:*
*"We know that our old man was crucified with him so that the body of sin would no longer dominate us, so that we would no longer be enslaved to sin" (Romans 6:6 NET)*

### *A Step to Consider:*
The next time I face the anxieties that life may bring my way, I will face them with a positive attitude and won't "LET THE OLD MAN IN!"

# Reflection 33

# *"Be the Living Expression of God's Kindness!"*

*March 23, 2024*

*"Let no one ever come to you without leaving better and happier. Be the living expression of God's kindness: kindness in your face, kindness in your eyes, kindness in your smile."*
— *Mother Teresa*

As we near the opening day of the Major League baseball season, I can often be seen with a smile on my face. I also notice smiles on the faces of many others as opening day approaches. The weather has certainly been teasing us, but it is the anticipation of the "new" season that spring training brings with it that truly inspires me. Hope may spring eternal in the early months of the Major League Baseball season.

Players getting one of their first MLB opportunities are significantly more likely to portray that big smile. One such player is the Atlanta Braves outfielder Forrest Wall who nervously answered a call from Braves manager Brian Snitker late this past Monday afternoon.

"My heart started going," Wall said. "I kind of knew the call was coming. I didn't know whether it would be good or bad. Then Snit had nothing but good things to say. He told me I had made the team. So, after that I was extremely thankful and excited. I was by myself in my car but so excited." How excited? "I was like yelling, 'Let's go!'" Wall said.

Wall spent the next few minutes sharing screams of joy with his wife, daughter, and parents, who truly appreciate the long journey that brought him to this first Opening Day roster selection. The 28-year-old outfielder is preparing for his 10th professional season, but his MLB experience only consists of the 15 games he played for Atlanta last year.

"You have so many tough conversations with these guys, when you can have one like that, I felt as good as he did, probably," Snitker said.

I've had the opportunity to reflect back over seven decades with regard to the things that have brought a smile to my face, and I'd like to share a couple in this reflection. The conversation Brian Snitker had with Forrest brought back some of the memories of anticipation I've experienced on this cancer journey of mine.

First, when I was a little boy, I remember my standard prayer at bedtime. I know it was meant to comfort, but one line always freaked me out!

"Now I lay me down to sleep. I pray the Lord my soul to keep. If I should die before I wake..."

Wait? What? If I should die before I wake? I think I will just stay awake for a while thank you very much!

Seven decades later that prayer makes a lot more sense. If I should die before I wake, I believe I will be in the presence of Jesus. I am not anxious to leave this life, but I am not afraid either.

I have had many loved ones who have gone home to heaven before me. I have also been blessed with some wonderful friends and colleagues who would likely say some nice things about me along with some funny and embarrassing stories.

I would like all of them to understand a very important truth. I learned some great lessons from my parents and others as I was growing up. But I can tell you with complete confidence that my life would most likely have gone off the rails without my relationship with Jesus. His love both restrained and sustained me. I believe my insecure and selfish heart would have taken me down a very different path without my faith, especially given the challenges of a cancer journey.

Any quality that you find positive in my life has been given or enhanced through my relationship with Jesus. Anytime I have disappointed or did not show love it was because I took my eyes off Him.

Paul writes:

> *"And now, dear brothers and sisters, one final*
> *thing. Fix your thoughts on what is true, and*

*honorable, and right, and pure, and lovely, and admirable. Think about things that are excellent and worthy of praise. Keep putting into practice all you learned and received from me—everything you heard from me and saw me doing. Then the God of peace will be with you"* (Philippians 4:8-9 NLT).

I know my heart. I know the crossroads I met in different seasons of my life, and how God gracefully and lovingly rescued me over and over. So, my message to all my friends and *"Home Team"* would be one of encouragement and hope.

As we near the end of the Lenten Season, while preparing for His glorious resurrection at Easter, remember, Jesus conquered death. He paid for our sins. It was the message of Christ that gave value to women, children, the poor, and the ignored. When you study His words and life you will see that many of His followers have fallen short, including me. Just as Forrest Wall "put in the work" to make the Atlanta Braves opening day roster, all that Jesus asks is that you accept Him in your heart as your Lord and Savior to become a part of His "team's roster!"

So, today's request would come out of deep love for you. Examine the claims of Jesus with an open heart and mind. Read the Gospel of John and ask for the Spirit to reveal truth to you. I certainly can't force you to follow Jesus, but I hope I have been a small influence for you to examine the life and claims of Jesus thoughtfully and honestly.

Following Jesus changed everything in my journey, and I would not be a good and loving friend if I did not share that with you. It may just bring a smile to your face, just as the smile and excitement Forrest Wall exhibited when he heard the news that he "made the team"!

As Mother Teresa writes:

> *"Let no one ever come to you without leaving better and happier. Be the living expression of God's kindness: kindness in your face, kindness in your eyes, kindness in your smile."* [35]

Having Jesus in your heart can make that kindness and smile happen!

### An Encouraging Attitude:
Having Jesus in your heart can make kindness and smiles happen!

### A Spiritual Insight:
*"And now, dear brothers and sisters, one final thing. Fix your thoughts on what is true, and honorable, and right, and pure, and lovely, and admirable. Think about things that are excellent and worthy of praise. Keep putting into practice all you learned and received from me—everything you heard from me and saw me doing. Then the God of peace will be with you"* (Philippians 4:8-9 NLT).

### A Step to Consider:
"Let no one ever come to you without leaving better and happier. Be the living expression of God's kindness: kindness in your face, kindness in your eyes, kindness in your smile." Mother Teresa

# Reflection 34

# *"Never Make Predictions,*
# *Especially About the Future"*

*April 20, 2024*

**"Never make predictions, especially about
the future."**

**Casey Stengel**

Whenever I stress about something that is off in the future, I remember something a good scouting friend said to me in the early days of my cancer journey. When so many thoughts and predictions were being channeled my way, he reminded me that "It's probably best to remember how bad we are at predicting the future."

The words resonated with me because they are so true. We so often are bad predictors of the future. We worry about something that never comes or isn't as bad as we predicted it would be. And it works on the "positive" side as well… We put off starting our exercise routine or beginning a big project until tomorrow because we think we'll feel more motivated then. I try my best to remember to stay in the present moment because I've found through my life experiences that just like one of my favorite baseball characters, Casey Stengel said, "Never make predictions, especially about the future." [36]

I just finished reading *Casey Stengel Baseball's Greatest Character* by Marty Appel. In his book, Appel paints an amazing portrait of Casey Stengel as the undisputed, quirky, hilarious, and beloved face of baseball. So many life lessons to be learned not only from Stengel, but from the game itself. It is a fun read about the man and the game he loved so much.

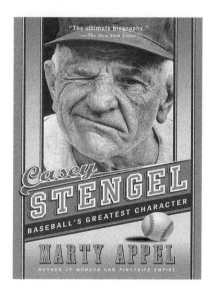

...and that brings me to today's reflection.

As a "long time" baseball scout and coach, I've come to realize that putting together a successful roster and team can often be difficult. A long season, especially at the professional level, can be a brutal grind. There can be lots of friction during that long regular season, and even the best teams can have embarrassing performances. Players and teams have hot and cold streaks. Obviously the most important ingredient is talent but there are a couple of other factors that help make a winning team.

One of the most important things that winning teams understand is that every teammate brings strengths and weaknesses to the team. A great team celebrates the strengths of each player and works together to offset the weaknesses. I pondered this as I was reading Marty Appel's book on Casey Stengel. Great managers and good teammates know that every player has strengths, and every player has weaknesses.

And that is the lesson I was thinking about for the Church. Too often we dwell on the weakness and not the gifts that God has given others. Or we acknowledge the gifts but make sure to note the weaknesses. All of us are a mix of gifts and flaws. The first mention of spiritual gifts is in Paul's letter to the Roman church.

> *"I long to see you so that I may impart to you some spiritual gift to make you strong— that is, that you and I may be mutually encouraged by each other's faith." (Romans 1:11)*

Paul wants to use our spiritual gifts to strengthen and encourage others. I believe that every single Christian is given spiritual gifts. We are given those gifts for many reasons but two of the primary ones are to glorify God and strengthen one another.

But I wonder if we sometimes look at our spiritual gifts as something that we exercise for our personal fulfillment. I am sure Casey Stengel at times "struck out" when his team needed his leadership. But his team and the rest of the league saw his gifts. That is what made him so valuable to his winning teams. His strengths were vital to the team winning. His flaws were compensated by the team working in unity toward the goal of the World Series.

Do we do that in the church? Or do we choose to focus on the flaws of others? The World Series is a wonderful goal, but it pales in comparison to the goal that Jesus challenged us to pursue. Do we understand what it means to be unified for the common goal expressed so succinctly in the Gospel of Matthew?

> *"Therefore, go and make disciples of all the nations, baptizing them in the name of the Father and the Son and the Holy Spirit. Teach these new disciples to obey all the commands I have given you. And be sure of this: I am with you always, even to the end of the age."*
> *Matthew 28:19-20*

That needs to be the game plan. Each of us has been given gifts to contribute. Each of us has flaws. Can we pray that we will be mature enough to focus on Who unites us instead of what divides us? Even one of the greatest managers in baseball had shortcomings. So will the pastor, elder, committee member, and volunteer as we pursue the Great Commission of Christ.

There is another thing that winning teams understand. You don't have to be best friends with everyone on the team, but you do have to be united for the common goal of the team. Jesus prayed for unity for those who follow Him.

*"May they experience such perfect unity that the world will know that you sent me and that you love them as much as you love me." John 17:23*

We have been given extraordinary gifts of grace, spiritual gifts, forgiveness, and partnership with the Father through Jesus. And then he outlines how we should respond in unity in this verse from 1 Corinthians.

*"I appeal to you, dear brothers and sisters, by the authority of our Lord Jesus Christ, to live in harmony with each other. Let there be no divisions in the church. Rather, be of one mind, united in thought and purpose." I Corinthians 1:10*

I lift up the following prayer as we work together to become united in thought and purpose to achieve this goal:

*"God give us the grace to be unified as a team for your glory. Teach us to use our gifts to strengthen one another and glorify you. Give us the strength to be a good teammate and the humility to believe that it cannot be about me for the team to succeed. Give me the desire to be a good teammate in the body of Christ. Teach me to see and exalt the gifts of my brothers and sisters even if they compete with my own talents. And especially teach me to be graceful with the flaws of others. We are all gifted and we are all flawed. A unified team understands that truth. Help us to do the same for the sake of the body of Christ."*

Let's all work to find a Church Community, wherever that may be, that will help support each other in this Great Commission. These things I pray in your name.

### *An Encouraging Attitude:*
One of the most important things that winning teams understand is that every teammate brings strengths and weaknesses to the team. A great team celebrates the strengths of each player and works together to offset the weaknesses.

### *A Spiritual Insight:*
*"I appeal to you, dear brothers and sisters, by the authority of our Lord Jesus Christ, to live in harmony with each other. Let there be no divisions in the church. Rather, be of one mind, united in thought and purpose." I Corinthians 1:10*

### *A Step to Consider:*
Let's all work to find a Church Community, wherever that may be, that will help support each other in this Great Commission.

# Reflection 35

# *"The Signs in Life that Bring us Hope"*

*May 5, 2024*

*"The day the Lord created hope was probably the same day he created Spring."*
*Bernard Williams*

Iowa's seasons can be brutal on plants and trees. Last summer the heat and lack of rain impacted many plants that I had put in the ground that spring and this past winter added to the struggle. As spring has sprung, I have been keeping a close eye on one of my favorite plants that lies along my morning walking trail. It is a lilac bush, and I wasn't sure that it made it through the winter.

Day after day the limbs were barren. Then one glorious day, tiny buds began to appear on the branches. Those green buds sprouted in defiance of summer and winters brutal assault until finally it blossomed in full color and wonderful fragrance. I stopped and dwelled on the miracle of life emerging out of barrenness as each day, the bush literally came to life. The beautiful lilac made me think of the words of Bernard Williams... "The day the Lord created hope was probably the same day he created Spring." I love that!

The brilliant colors and smells that spring provides brings joy to my heart, kind of like the joy I often experience with new puppies and the game of baseball!

Is there anything more hopeful than watching the beauty of budding leaves and blooming flowers turning the melancholy of winter into a wondrous palette of invigorating colors? Every spring is a reminder that God will bring beauty from darkness and life from death.

Our world can often seem to be in a state of perpetual winter. As I watch troubling events, both here and abroad, it brings me back to some lessons my parents taught me, and hopefully, in turn, I passed onto my children. Those lessons were reinforced in a recent episode of the Andy Griffith Show which I always watched as a kid and often spent time with my mother enjoying episodes on MeTV in mom's later years.

In this particular episode, when Buddy Ebsen told Andy he should just let Opie "decide for himself" how he wanted to live... Andy had these words of wisdom.

> *"No, I'm afraid it don't work that way. You can't let a young'n decide for himself. He'll grab at the first flashy thing with shiny ribbons on it. Then, when he finds out there's a hook in it, it's too late. Wrong ideas come packaged with so much glitter that it's hard to convince 'em that other things might be better in the long run. All a parent can do is say 'wait' and 'trust me' and try to keep temptation away."* [37]

Somehow... I believe we are losing this basic truth in today's society.

I can remember as a child being reminded, often in not so gentle terms, that when you're a child you will go through life learning, failing, succeeding, and making mistakes. In that time, you'll also think you know everything, but you actually know very little! Yep, I certainly experienced that, and my own life experience has taught me some wisdom I wish I had in those early years... Maybe it has for you as well. I've learned to enjoy the journey, and welcome the adventure because as a cancer survivor, I know it can always change in a blink!

During the times I have felt "lost", going through that learning, failing, and making mistakes time in my life, and as I think of those who are currently discontent, making poor choices in real time, it reminds me of the parable of the lost sheep...

Jesus reminds us in that parable that every one of us is so precious to Him. He loves us so much and He will never give up on us, no matter what! He leaves the ninety-nine that are safe to go to find that one lost little sheep because that sheep is so important to Him, just like each of us.

For followers of Jesus, we see signs of life even in the darkness. Like that bit of green emerging from what appeared to be a lifeless branch and ultimately turned into the beautiful lilac, we too can have hope this spring!

Nothing we do for the Lord is ever useless. Nothing! And even as we face the reality of a dangerous world, we know we have the twin promise of victory over sin and death through Jesus. So as spring continues, lets choose to marvel at the renewing of life and the hope that holds for all of us. Paul wrote about this miracle in 2 Corinthians.

> *"Therefore, if anyone is in Christ, he is a new creation. The old has passed away; behold, the new has come." 2 Corinthians 5:17*

We have become new creations now and forever in Jesus. Doesn't that hope feel especially good this spring? On many days we may feel the struggle, but Jesus guarantees one day we will "bloom" for eternity.

### *An Encouraging Attitude:*
We have become new creations now and forever in Jesus. Doesn't that hope feel especially good this spring? On many days we may feel the struggle, but Jesus guarantees one day we will "bloom" for eternity.

### *A Spiritual Insight:*
*"Therefore, if anyone is in Christ, he is a new creation. The old has passed away; behold, the new has come." 2 Corinthians 5:17*

### *A Step to Consider:*
Nothing we do for the Lord is ever useless. Nothing! And even as we face the reality of a dangerous world, we know we have the twin promise of victory over sin and death through Jesus.

So as spring continues, lets choose to marvel at the renewing of life and the hope that holds for all of us.

# Reflection 36

# *"Seeking the 'Touch of the Master'"*

### *May 20, 2024*

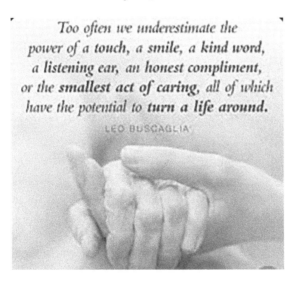

> Too often we underestimate the power of a touch, a smile, a kind word, a listening ear, an honest compliment, or the **smallest act of caring**, all of which have the potential to **turn a life around.**
>
> LEO BUSCAGLIA

*...May we all seek not only the 'Touch of the Master', but also seek out others with a kind smile, a kind word, a listening ear, or an honest compliment.*

I have been doing some reading as of late given the fact that several of my close friends are having battles with some very serious health-related issues... Reading helps me process and offers my mind positive escapes from the anxiety I face when dealing with life challenges. Those of you who know me, also know I have been a dog lover all my life. I have owned several Labradors over the years, and always enjoy a good story about dogs. I turned to one of my favorite authors, Dave Burchett and his book titled *Stay: Lessons My Dogs Taught Me about Life, Loss and Grace.*

A passage in the book really touched my heart, and provided some good perspective as I process what my close friends and their families are experiencing now on their life journeys. Like many of my friends, including myself, we all will face the reality at some point in our lives of "nearing home".

The passage in Dave Burchett's book *Stay: Lessons My Dogs Taught Me about Life, Loss and Grace,* reads as follows:

> *"A sick man turned to his doctor, as he was preparing to leave the examination room and said, "Doctor, I am afraid to die. Tell me what lies on the other side."*
>
> *Very quietly, the doctor said, 'I don't know.'*
>
> *"You don't know? You, a Christian man, do not know what is on the other side?"*
>
> *The doctor was holding the handle of the door; on the other side of which came a sound of scratching and whining, and as he opened the door, a dog sprang into the room and leaped on him with an eager show of gladness.*
>
> *Turning to the patient, the doctor said, 'Did you notice my dog? He's never been in this room before. He didn't know what was inside. He knew nothing except that his master was here, and when the door opened, he sprang in without*

*fear. I know little of what is on the other side
of death, but I do know one thing… I know my
Master is there and that is enough.'"* [38]

I love that thought!

A personal story of story of mine that applies here is a story about one of my Labrador retrievers, one of my first, who grew up with me and my family out on the farm. Her name was Josie, and she was a lovable pup who liked to explore the farm, it's fields and a creek that ran through the property we were living on at that time.

One day, she went missing which was very unusual, so we searched the nearby fields and farms looking for her. We left messages with neighbors to no avail. After about a week, a neighbor contacted me to share they found a dog in one of their outbuildings. She was still alive but had a conibear trap wrapped around her neck on which she had apparently chewed through the chain that had secured the trap, and in turn, dragged herself inside the building. She was emaciated but clinging to life. Someone had apparently been trapping our creek illegally when Josie stumbled onto one.

I gathered Josie up after removing the conibear trap that was squeezing her neck and sat her in the front seat of my truck, wrapped her in a blanket and ran her into our veterinarian to see if he could help her. The veterinarian was able to help in treating her wounds and provided a place for her to remain for a few days as she recovered and gained some strength back.

The vet did a masterful job treating Josie and helping her regain some strength. My "spiritual epiphany" occurred when I was called to the animal hospital to pick Josie up. I waited as the staff brought Josie out. She shuffled slowly out, and I was taken aback by her appearance. Josie was trembling, frightened, and appeared to be in some pain. Her head was down, and her perpetual motion tail was strangely still. She seemed confused and disoriented. Then I walked over to Josie and simply touched her. Almost immediately she quit trembling, and she made a valiant attempt to wag her tail. I carefully got her into my truck and took Josie home to heal.

As I reflect on that scene, it struck me that Josie's reaction to my touch and mere presence was a wonderful illustration of how Jesus comforts, or desires to comfort, me when I face difficult times. When I (her master) touched Josie, she was comforted. Her pain was not gone. She was still a bit disoriented and unsure. Josie's circumstances hadn't really changed at all. But she knew that her master was there and that made it better.

What a picture that is of how the "Touch of Jesus" enables us to respond when we are frightened, in pain, disoriented and confused. We need to remind ourselves that Jesus never promised that all trouble would vanish when we believe in Him. In fact, the opposite often happens. Jesus did promise that He would be there and that would be enough.

My hope not only for myself, but for all, is that we will seek, realize, and be comforted by the "touch of the Master" in times of difficulty. Paul realized that contentment is not found in good circumstances. He wrote these words from prison while chained to a Roman soldier.

> *"I rejoice greatly in the Lord that at last you have renewed your concern for me. Indeed, you have been concerned, but you had no opportunity to show it. I am not saying this because I am in need, for I have learned to be content whatever the circumstances. I know what it is to be in need, and I know what it is to have plenty. I have learned the secret of being content in any and every situation, whether well fed or hungry, whether living in plenty or in want" (Philippians 4, The Message).*

I am so grateful that Paul did not write I "am" content and I "know" the secret. He was divinely inspired to honestly write that he had "learned" to be content and he had "learned" the secret of being content. It did not come naturally or easily to Paul either.

I believe we may all be desiring the "Touch of the Master" and that we are always learning as well. Our nature is to typically not enjoy the moment at hand and the blessings that usually surround us. Satan would have us living in regret of the past and fear of the future. Jesus said to follow Him. He told us our past is forgiven and our future is in His Hands. Let's enjoy the moment, while seeking the "Touch of the Master" as we continue to learn to be content. It can be life changing!

One of my close friends shared that he often struggles being able to bring himself back to the present moment and can get frustrated with how many times throughout the day he often must do so. My response: Join the club. This is something I too need to do often during the day as well. I've spent years grabbing onto thoughts and emotions that came into my head... and as a retired Principal, there have been a few! It's going to take time to get into a different habit.

As Leo Buscaglia, a former Special Education instructor, speaker and author in the Department of Special Education at the University of Southern California, shares:

> *"Too often we underestimate the power of a touch, a smile, a kind word, a listening ear, an honest compliment, or the smallest act of caring, all of which have the potential to turn a life around."* [39]

May we all seek not only the "Touch of the Master", but also seek out others with a kind smile, a kind word, a listening ear, or an honest compliment as we all will face the reality at some point in our lives of "nearing home".

### *An Encouraging Attitude:*
It struck me that Josie's reaction to my touch and mere presence was a wonderful illustration of how Jesus comforts, or desires to comfort, me when I face difficult times. When I (her master)

touched Josie, she was comforted. Her pain was not gone. She was still a bit disoriented and unsure. Josie's circumstances hadn't really changed at all. But she knew that her master was there and that made it better.

### A Spiritual Insight:
*"I rejoice greatly in the Lord that at last you have renewed your concern for me. Indeed, you have been concerned, but you had no opportunity to show it. I am not saying this because I am in need, for I have learned to be content whatever the circumstances. I know what it is to be in need, and I know what it is to have plenty. I have learned the secret of being content in any and every situation, whether well fed or hungry, whether living in plenty or in want." (Philippians 4, The Message)*

### A Step to Consider:
"Too often we underestimate the power of a touch, a smile, a kind word, a listening ear, an honest compliment, or the smallest act of caring, all of which have the potential to turn a life around."

# Reflection 37

## *"Picking Up the Pieces"*

*June 30, 2024*

*"I'll ask for a brain instead of a heart," said the Scarecrow, — "because a fool wouldn't know what to do with a heart, even if he had one." "I'll take the heart," replied the tin man, "because intelligence doesn't make a person happy, and happiness is the most beautiful thing in the world."*

*The Wizard of Oz.*

One of the biggest hurdles I had to clear in my own mind before starting my Reflections from the Home Team blog was getting past the question: Who am I to think anyone would want to hear what I have to say? What qualifies me to write about the things that I have tried to process on my personal life's journey? And what have I really accomplished through that process?

Simply put, I've come to realize that the many conversations I've had with others who have been experiencing similar challenges, the "mess" those challenges have created in their lives, the worst things they've experienced, and the things they're most embarrassed by are exactly the things that qualified "us" to speak to others. It reminds me that the things we struggle with, the flaws we think we have, the mistakes we've made are exactly the things that can allow us to help others.

Rather than be ashamed of them, limited by them, or hiding them from view, we can instead use them to help provide some positivity and support in the lives of others. This is not something where we must be perfect in life. In fact, our greatest "mess" may be the very thing that qualifies us the most to help other people. And that brings to mind a couple thoughts I'd like to share in this reflection as we reach the midpoint of summer.

I ran across a quote this past week when doing some reading that certainly reflects where we are these days as a society given the divisiveness we are experiencing in our country today. It reads:

> *"Negative People Offer a Problem for Every Solution..."*

Albert Einstein is generally credited for the thought. If so, this may be his best theory! I have certainly reached my fill on negative discourse. It seems our leaders on both sides, the media, and social media platforms spend a ridiculous percentage of their energy on what is wrong with this world instead of ways to address those problems with a solution. Their solutions often include condemnation, judgement, and the dismissal of people who simply ask questions... looking for solutions! Perhaps the most distressing thing for me is that many in the church have fallen into the same dark space. Christian social media responses to cultural and doctrinal issues may be slightly less profane but not much, if any, less negative.

For the record, I am willing to have thoughtful discussions about tough issues. But I am done with the negativity being peddled by so many others and it is not because I am naive about the condition of the world. I am done with the negativity precisely because of the condition of the world... This hurting world and country of ours needs hope, light, and grace. We need thoughtful listeners with a message of love. We need the positive message of the Good News. I hope to continue to bring some positivity with my thoughts as I feel quite comfortable that the negative side will be well represented by countless others.

Every day we get to make choices....

We can be judgmental, or we can be joyful.

We can be pessimistic, or we can be prayerful.

We can be condemning, or we can be caring.

We can be fearful, or we can be faithful.

We can be grace-filled, or we can be graceless.

We as Christians are supposed to be a positive light in this world, but please don't take my word for it. Your argument may be with Jesus!

> *"In the same way, let your good deeds shine out for all to see, so that everyone will praise your heavenly Father" (Matthew 5:16, NLT).*

What I see too often is this very sad paraphrase of His words demonstrated through social media platforms. "Let my sharp words shame or demean you so that everyone will see how clever I am and praise me." Paul addressed why we should be eager to be a positive light in the world.

> *"For once you were full of darkness, but now you have light from the Lord. So, live as people of light! "Ephesians 5:8.*

My heart breaks when I see how many followers of Christ seem to have forgotten they were once full of darkness. It is only because of God's grace that we have light.

Perhaps we could take a little advice from the tin man in *The Wizard of Oz...*

> *"I'll ask for a brain instead of a heart," said the Scarecrow, — "because a fool wouldn't know what to do with a heart, even if he had one." "I'll take the heart," replied the tin man, "because intelligence doesn't make a person happy, and happiness is the most beautiful thing in the world." The Wizard of Oz.* [40]

Instead of using our "intelligence" to manufacture sharp words to shame or demean others so that everyone will see how clever we are, it would be best to use our hearts to seek to understand and love one another, even with our differences by living out the truth of John 13:35.

> *"Your love for one another will prove to the world that you are my disciples." John 13:35*

That response just isn't natural my friends... That is a mindset based on who God is. The choice to love and be light is infinitely more important than winning online arguments, getting social media likes, and racking up followers. My belief is there is nothing more important than wanting to be a loving light for the Good News of the Gospel.

A good friend recently shared a post from author John Roedell which talks about what happens when you have a conversation with God and He writes back, providing hope when life's circumstances may be causing you to fall apart. Been there a few times myself... how about you? It reads:

Me: Hey God.

God: Hello...

Me: I'm falling apart. Can you put me back together?

God: I would rather not.

Me: Why?

God: Because you aren't a puzzle.

Me: What about all the pieces of my life that are falling onto the ground?

God: Let them stay there for a while. They fell off for a reason. Take some time and decide if you need any of those pieces back.

Me: You don't understand! I'm breaking down!

God: No— you don't understand. You are breaking through. What you are feeling are just growing pains. You are shedding the things and the people in your life that are holding you back. You aren't falling apart. You are falling into place. Relax. Take some deep breaths and allow those things you don't need any more to fall off you. Quit holding onto the pieces that don't fit you anymore. Let them fall off. Let them go.

Me: Once I start doing that, what will be left of me?

God: Only the very best pieces of you.

Me: I'm scared of changing.

God: I keep telling you: YOU AREN'T CHANGING! YOU ARE BECOMING!

Me: Becoming who?

God: Becoming who I created you to be! A person of light and love and charity and hope and courage and joy and mercy and grace and compassion. I made you for more than the shallow pieces you have decided to adorn yourself with that you cling to with such greed and fear. Let those things fall off you. I love you! Don't change! Become! Become! Become who I made you to be. I'm going to keep telling you this until you remember it.

Me: There goes another piece.

God: Yep. Let it be.

Me: So... I'm not broken?

God: Of course not! But you are breaking like the dawn. It's a new day!

John Roedel [41]

May we each become a person of light, love, charity, hope, courage, joy, mercy, grace, and compassion as we become what God intends us to be!

### *An Encouraging Attitude:*
This hurting world and country of ours needs hope, light, and grace. We need thoughtful listeners with a message of love. We

228

need the positive message of the Good News. I hope to continue to bring some positivity with my thoughts as I feel quite comfortable that the negative side will be well represented by countless others.

## *A Spiritual Insight:*
*"Your love for one another will prove to the world that you are my disciples." John 13:35*

## *A Step to Consider:*
May we each become a person of light, love, charity, hope, courage, joy, mercy, grace, and compassion as we become what God intends us to be!

# Reflection 38

# *"Making a Difficult Challenge Productive"*

*July 6, 2024*

THIS FALLEN TREE REFUSED TO DIE, INSTEAD GREW 4 MORE TREES OUT OF ITSELF.

THIS IS WHAT HAPPENS WHEN YOU DON'T QUIT!

*I believe that difficult circumstances help to "grow" us in our faith. The cancer journey has given me many opportunities to reevaluate priorities in my relationship with God and others. The frightening uncertainty of a cancer journey has also allowed me the opportunity to show how faith makes a difference in crisis, and that God can make even our life's most difficult challenges into something productive!*

R ecently, I have had several friends who have been diagnosed with cancer, all at different stages, so I thought I'd share a few thoughts about coping... something we all must do when faced with life challenges.

Cancer most certainly is a life-changing event... From receiving the news of a diagnosis to understanding the treatment plan, those diagnosed with cancer go through many kinds of emotions along with physical discomfort resulting from treatment options such as chemotherapy, and radiation therapy, both of which I have experienced. My friends have shared they are experiencing pain and fatigue, appetite changes, and memory changes all of which can have an overwhelming impact on their mental fitness in addition to the physical challenges they will experience. So... How do you cope? Well, I'm certainly no expert, but I can definitely speak from experience!

I recall feeling overwhelmed once I received my diagnosis, which made it hard to go about my daily activities, and in turn created quite a bit of anxiety and even some depression. However, depression was the opposite of what my mind and body needed during that time. In order to overcome the hurdles that my treatments created, it was vital to have optimism and determination to beat the diagnosis.

Maintaining a positive mindset helped provide me with the strength, hope, and resilience I needed during those difficult times. It allowed me to focus on possibilities, maintain a sense of control, and foster and internalize the belief that I could fight and win over this disease! Embracing positivity helped me reduce stress, anxiety, and depression, while promoting my overall emotional well-being. A bit of a stubborn attitude I developed over my athletic career about *Never Giving Up* also may have helped!

# NEVER GIVE UP!

I must share that I am also a follower of Christ, and that my belief system was initially challenged when I received my diagnosis... Questions kept popping into my mind... Why me? Why now? What have I done to deserve this? I prayed that the Lord would provide some answers. Well, I kept waiting, and waiting as I prepared to begin treatments.

About a week after being diagnosed, out of the blue, I got an email from a dear College friend that I had not heard from in about 25 years. She asked if I was the same David Welter who attended Cornell College in the late 1970's and I shared, "yes, that's me!" She then asked, "Do you know how many David Welter's there are in this world?" I said no that I'd never really checked... Then she shared that she had a dream the previous night, having traveled back to Cornell in that dream, and couldn't find me there. I told her that is ironic because I have just been diagnosed with cancer and given a 50/50 chance of survival...

We had a good chat over email, and I found that she was a practicing OT out on the West Coast, that she was a Christian and that we both believed in the power of dreams. To make a long story short, Becky provided me wonderful guidance as

I went through treatments both physically as well as spiritually. For me, that was part of my answer from the Lord and reinforced the fact that establishing support and good communication are essential ingredients in winning the battle. It also strengthened my belief that the Lord provides answers to prayer, maybe not in our preferred time frame, but rather in His!

Being in community with others means you share their joys and their sorrows. Sometimes the sorrows come in tsunami waves and all you can do is care, pray, and be present. Jesus told His followers that we are to be a light to those around us.

> *"You are the light of the world—like a city on a hilltop that cannot be hidden. No one lights a lamp and then puts it under a basket. Instead, a lamp is placed on a stand, where it gives light to everyone in the house. In the same way, let your good deeds shine out for all to see, so that everyone will praise your heavenly Father"* *(Matthew 5:14-16).*

I don't know about you, but those challenges from Jesus can feel daunting. Sometimes I don't feel much like a light to the world... I feel more like the dimmest bulb in the lighting department at Menards. A quote from Phillip Yancy helps put it in perspective for me.

> *"Imperfection is the only prerequisite for grace. Light only gets in through the cracks."* *Philip Yancey* [42]

For years I tried to patch those cracks of imperfection with self-effort when faced with the challenges a cancer journey can bring. Now I own each and every flaw and crack that allows the light of the Gospel into my heart. And when I am in community with others, (my beloved Home Team) my hope is that they see that light shining right back through those same cracks of imperfection.

Suddenly, the command of Jesus is not so daunting because it has NOTHING to do with me. It is all about letting the light of the Gospel into my heart and sharing that light with others. Then good deeds flow out of gratitude and not begrudging obligation. So... Let it Shine!

I believe that God uses difficult circumstances to grow us in our faith. The cancer journey has given me many opportunities to reevaluate priorities in my relationship with God and others. The frightening uncertainty of a cancer journey has also allowed me the opportunity to show how faith makes a difference in crisis, and that God can make even our life's most difficult challenges into something productive!

I used to get angry, and at times judgmental when those who identify as Christians didn't live up to their title. Now I mainly feel sad at missed opportunities to show how Jesus can make a difference when we trust Him during the trials that come our way. Christians should have a message of hope during what can often be a confusing and anxious time in our lives. By demonstrating that trusting God gives peace and hope in difficult times, we can provide a comforting message to those dealing with those challenges.

Let's remember where our light comes from and pray that we can be a light shining for others this week. Let your good deeds reflect the loving light of our Father. You might be amazed how much of a difference that can make!

### An Encouraging Attitude:

Maintaining a positive mindset helped provide me with the strength, hope, and resilience I needed during those difficult times. It allowed me to focus on possibilities, maintain a sense of control, and foster and internalize the belief that I could fight and win over this disease! Embracing positivity helped me reduce stress, anxiety, and depression, while promoting my overall emotional well-being. A bit of a stubborn attitude I developed over my athletic career about *Never Giving Up* also may have helped!

### A Spiritual Insight:

*"You are the light of the world—like a city on a hilltop that cannot be hidden. No one lights a lamp and then puts it under a basket. Instead, a lamp is placed on a stand, where it gives light to everyone in the house. In the same way, let your good deeds shine out for all to see, so that everyone will praise your heavenly Father"* (Matthew 5:14-16).

### A Step to Consider:

Let's remember where our light comes from and pray that we can be a light shining for others. Let your good deeds reflect the loving light of our Father. You might be amazed how much of a difference that can make!

# Reflection 39

# *"Real Friends Are a Treasure!"*

## *July 17, 2024*

*...All friends are a blessing. Real friends are a treasure, and those friends are good for the heart and soul!*

Today, I want to share some thoughts about a close friend who continues to impact my life from Heaven... His name is Wade Olson, and he passed unexpectantly earlier this spring. As I gain more miles on my life odometer, I seem to reflect more and more about when it becomes my time to exit this world. The shooting of our former President this past week was a shock to many…including me. We need to be praying for all those impacted by the shooting and their families. But one truth is often overlooked when tragedies like this happen. It's this: you and I are always just an inch away from eternity. As has been made very clear, if that shot had been one inch closer, it could have been the difference between a flesh wound and a death wound. In the same way you and I are always an inch away from death, probably not from a bullet, but from a prognosis, a heart attack, or a car accident…

Over the years, I have been blessed with many friends who have shown me what friendship truly means. The irony is that one of the men who continues to show me what it means to have a sincere and true friendship is now living in the eternal company of Jesus. He showed me that true friendship is living your life in a way that shows the love and grace of Jesus.

If I wrote the impact of my friend Wade's impact had on me, it would make this a very long read so I decided to reflect on several things that resonate in my heart consistently and powerfully about Wade. His loss as a close friend is still hard for me to navigate, but I feel the urge today to share some thoughts about our friendship.

Wade passed away unexpectedly this spring following a heart procedure at Mayo Clinic. Wade's life journey demonstrated to me that you need to make choices when life takes a tough turn. You can either quit or you can live fully in each moment for as long as you can. I often witnessed Wade showing up for events and activities when he clearly did not feel his best. But he showed up with joy in his heart and spirit, particularly when we went fishing together, or were working as colleagues with students and staff at Holmes Jr. High! We often discussed scripture and its influence on many of the decisions we made. One of our favorite verses is found in 1 Thessalonians.

> *"Always be joyful. Never stop praying. Be thankful in all circumstances, for this is God's will for you who belong to Christ Jesus" (1 Thessalonians 5:15-18, NLT).*

Wade not only shared his love of that verse, but he also lived it!

A memory that I will always cherish about Wade is what happened every single time I saw him. Wade would smile his warm smile, then look into my eyes and ask, "how are you doing?" The difference with Wade was that he really meant that question. If you needed three hours to tell him what was going on he would never glance at his watch, and he would listen. We have been close friends since meeting in a Bible Study many years ago, and then in turn, spending 16 years as colleagues at Holmes Junior High.

Wade was the kind of friend that was good for my heart and my soul. The advent of social media has certainly accentuated the difference between friends and friendships. I have many Facebook "friends," befriended with a click. It's easy to have friends who know what you like, listen to, and read. But it is hard work and risky to cultivate friendships with people who know who you are when the exterior breaks down.

Real friends are a treasure, and at times, I have not priori-tized the importance of building real friendships. In the grand scheme of life, we will generally just have a handful of real friends. Friends who you can tell anything to, say anything to and not be rejected. Friends who will drop everything when you need them. It certainly can be a risk to allow others to see whom we really are, and it can only happen in a relationship centered on trust and grace. Wade was just that type of friend. Wade had a heart for serving others, especially his family, and that made a huge impact on my heart.

As mentioned earlier, we often discussed scripture and a verse from John 13 best describes the way Wade lived his life.

*"So now I am giving you a new commandment:*
*Love each other. Just as I have loved you, you*
*should love each other."* John 13:34 *NLT*

Wade lived that command by being there to help others without fanfare. He passed away following his surgery, but that verse reflects one of his qualities that will stick with me until my time comes. When someone or something needed his assistance, if he could be of help, he didn't need to think or pray about it, he just did it!

When we honestly ask ourselves which person in our lives means the most to us, we often find that it is those who, instead of giving much advice, solutions, or cures, have chosen rather to share our pain and touch our wounds with a gentle and tender hand. The friend who can be silent with us in a moment of despair or confusion, who can stay with us in an hour of grief and bereavement, who can tolerate not knowing, not healing and face with us the reality of our powerlessness, that is a friend who cares. ...and to me, that was Wade Olson.

I look forward to reuniting with Wade and the many more family and friends who have passed before me someday. What a glorious *HOPE* to have as we endure both the good and challenging things that life on this earth "pitches our way!" My hope is that Wade and those many other family and friends who are now in Heaven will save me a spot on the bench in our *Eternal Dugout* with our Lord and Savior Jesus Christ.

I also pray that God will use the tragedy that took place this past week as a spiritual wake up call to millions of Americans as to the brevity of life, surety of death and urgency of salvation. My prayer is that it is a wakeup call for us all.

Rest in Peace my friend! You will be missed...

### An Encouraging Attitude:
...All friends are a blessing. Real friends are a treasure, and those friends are good for the heart and soul!

### A Spiritual Insight:
*"So now I am giving you a new commandment: Love each other. Just as I have loved you, you should love each other."* John 13:34 *NLT*

## *A Step to Consider:*

When we honestly ask ourselves which person in our lives means the most to us, we often find that it is those who, instead of giving much advice, solutions, or cures, have chosen rather to share our pain and touch our wounds with a gentle and tender hand. The friend who can be silent with us in a moment of despair or confusion, who can stay with us in an hour of grief and bereavement, who can tolerate not knowing, not healing and face with us the reality of our powerlessness, that is a friend who cares...

# Reflection 40

# *"The More Love You Give the More Love You Will Have"*

*August 4, 2024*

*"In the kingdom of love there is no competition; there is no possessiveness or control. The more love you give away, the more love you will have."*

*–John O'Donohue, Celtic Poet* [44]

I've been so very blessed to be able to spend precious time with my grandchildren over the years, and I've often asked myself how can I, as a loving grandparent, make an eternal impact on their lives? I think back to my own children's grandparents who so lovingly cared for them as they were growing up.

There is a well-known saying that states people may not remember for what you said or did, but they will always remember the way you made them feel... More than their accomplishments, people are truly remembered for their acts of kindness, expressions of gratitude, and unwavering attitude of thankfulness. I can honestly say that my children's grandparents will always be remembered by them for the way they made them feel loved and appreciated. I'm hopeful my precious little ones will someday feel the same about me.

Several years ago, I was part of a small study group that met regularly and during one session everyone was asked this question: what person had the biggest impact on you spiritually growing up? Three-quarters of our group shared the same answer. A grandparent. I was one of those who gave that response. My life has always been impacted then and to this day by my dear mother, Rita, grandmother to my three adult children.

So many words come to mind as I remember "Gramma Rita". The first word is always gratitude. Anytime I visited, she was grateful for one minute of my time or for many hours. She was grateful for everything and everyone. Another word is joy. Gramma Rita always had a ready and sometimes mischievous smile that cheered me constantly through the trials of growing up and well into my adult years. She was my champion and she never once showed disappointment in me.

She had almost no formal education, having graduated with a high school class of seven in the tiny Northeast Iowa town of North Washington, yet she was one of the wisest women I have ever known. I remember her lamenting once about my cancer journey and that she wished she was smarter so she could understand the words used to describe the ups and downs of my cancer journey better. The conversation often turned to our faith and its importance in our lives, me with my cancer diagnosis, and her as she neared coming closer to being reunited with her husband of over 60 years, my father Bob, who was waiting for her in Heaven.

But few other people I have met have allowed God's Word to penetrate their heart and actions more than my mother Rita, Gramma to my three children. She was my first messenger of grace, although I did not realize that until later in life. She modeled unconditional love through some very difficult seasons, no matter how I responded during that time I never once felt guilty or unloved in her presence. That was grace in real life. To this day, I think of her grace filled responses whenever I feel ungrateful for some real or perceived slight.

That was no accident. Mom was a woman who was dialed into her love and commitment for each of us, her children, and in turn for her grandkids. She demonstrated that God knows our needs and that He moves, most often before we have any idea. It gave me a very early and unforgettable example of how God provides. I have never forgotten that lesson. When I face uncertainty, I know that He provides, in part because of a five-foot-five dynamo of faith who showed me what faith and grace look like in my daily journey.

Isn't it interesting how a simple person of faith, kindness, joy, and grace can have such an influence? She knows I loved her, but she had no idea how much her walk with Jesus affected me. Part of that is because I didn't recognize it myself until later in life and I can't wait to tell her in Heaven someday.

Proverbs 17:6 says that "Grandchildren are the crowning glory of the aged". Amen to that! What a wonderful gift from God to have the opportunity to love, care, and share your life with these precious little ones. We can have a unique connection and voice to our grandkids. I share the hope of John who wrote these words.

> *I could have no greater joy than to hear that my children (and grandchildren) are following the truth. (3 John 3:4, NLT)*

I'm hopeful I am having such an impact in my beloved grandkids lives. I won't know the whole story on this earth, but I will do my best to show them the love and grace of Jesus. Billy Graham may have summed up my goal perfectly.

> *"The greatest legacy one can pass on to one's children and grandchildren is not money or*

> *other material things accumulated in one's life,*
> *but rather a legacy of character and faith."* [45]

May we all leave such a legacy! A great grandparent is also a grateful grandparent... Now, this grandpa has got some thank you notes I need to go write in appreciation to my children and grandchildren for giving me such an opportunity to love, care, and share my life with them. After all, there is no better feeling than hearing... "I love you, Papa!"

### An Encouraging Attitude:
There is a well-known saying that states people may not remember for what you said or did, but they will always remember the way you made them feel... More than their accomplishments, people are truly remembered for their acts of kindness, expressions of gratitude, and unwavering attitude of thankfulness.

### A Spiritual Insight:
*I could have no greater joy than to hear that my children (and grandchildren) are following the truth. (3 John 3:4, NLT)*

### A Step to Consider:
"The greatest legacy one can pass on to one's children and grandchildren is not money or other material things accumulated in one's life, but rather a legacy of character and faith."

# Reflection 41

# *"Perseverance and Endurance"*

*August 11, 2024*

*As the three United States Women Gymnasts took the stand in Paris to receive their Olympic medals, I noted that the podium had a gold medalist, who had mental health struggles and the twisties, a silver medalist who's had not one, not two, but three ACL tears, and a bronze medalist who is in remission from kidney disease! A true representation of perseverance and endurance!*

I've spent some time this past week viewing some amazing performances by athletes from around the World in the 2024 Olympic games being held in Paris. After the somewhat controversial opening ceremonies, things got back to what they are intended to be in the 2024 Olympic games.

The Olympics have become a significant global event fostering international cooperation, competition, and cultural exchanges after originating in Olympia, Greece in the 8th Century BC. The games have undergone a number of changes since then, with the so called "modern games" taking place in Athens beginning in 1896. The enjoyable part for me in this year's Olympic Games has been watching competitors from different countries embrace the spirit of competition as well as each other after each event. It is truly what athletics and competition should be about!

The 16 days of the Paris 2024 Olympics encapsulated some human drama, the iconic, historic, and mesmeric venues of France's capital, sport-celebrity mash ups accompanied by a soundtrack of anthems bonding together fans and athletes alike. Even though I've had enough of Snoop Dogg for a while, I have to admit, Celine Dion halfway up the Eiffel Tower singing the French crowd's favorite "Hymne à l'amour", was quite memorable.

So, from 2024 in Paris, to the handover of the Olympic Games to Los Angeles in 2028 we will go, but not without some memories I will carry with me from this year's Olympic Games. One thing in particular stood out to me as I watched one of the medal ceremonies for Women's Gymnastics.

As the three United States Women Gymnasts took the stand in Paris to receive their Olympic medals, I noted that the podium had a gold medalist, who had mental health struggles and the twisties, a silver medalist who's had not one, not two, but three ACL tears, and a bronze medalist who is in remission from kidney disease!

Such a great example that when we run into problems and trials, we can know that they help us develop endurance. And endurance develops strength of character, and character strengthens our confidence to accomplish the goals we set out to achieve! Congratulations to our United States 2024 Women's Olympic Gymnasts!

As Paul writes in Romans…

> *"We can rejoice too, when we run into problems and trials, for we know that they help us develop endurance. And endurance develops strength of character, and character strengthens our confident hope of salvation. And this hope will not lead to disappointment." Romans 5:3-5 NLT*

The trials these young ladies experienced along the way to their Olympic success reminds me that difficulties in our lives often are part of God's errands for each of us. When we are sent on them, it is not a sign of His distaste for our company, but of His confidence in us. The question is, are we confident in Him?

Are there ups and downs in the Christian life? Absolutely. Will friends sometimes drop you, or shoot arrows through your heart? Yes, they will. Will there come tests of your faith when feelings must be shunned and only your foundational faith will sustain you? You bet! That is when the endurance, perseverance, and positivity these young athletes displayed on their way to the medal rounds comes into play.

If you or someone you love is battling cancer, serious illness, depression, grief or loss, the lessons displayed by these young American athletes of perseverance and endurance will help provide encouragement for the journey they may be on. As demonstrated by these young women: ATTITUDE MAKES A DIFFERENCE!

We have all seen it – the attitude that turns an athlete into a champion, that turns an ordinary soldier into a hero, that turns an entertainer into a star, that turns a failure into an honorable legacy. Those of us who are close to cancer and its survivors see it every day as well. We see the attitudes that turn wounded sufferers into survivors.

I know as well as anyone that attitude isn't everything. It won't turn a couch potato into a world-class athlete or an off-key singer into a superstar. As important as attitude is, some patients with inspiring, positive attitudes will succumb to their illnesses while others with negative attitudes will survive. I've witnessed it... I do know however that having come face to face with cancer in my own life, that I approach life with a different attitude. I have come to realize that life is short and what I do with the time that I have is important.

For me, cancer sounded an alarm that caused me to react and take action so that I can give the greatest amount of attention to things that really matter. I'm certainly not perfect, but my goal is to make every moment count, and to learn the lessons that each day brings.

One of those lessons is...

> *"Cancer is so limited ...It cannot cripple Love. It cannot shatter Hope. It cannot corrode Faith. It cannot destroy Peace. It cannot kill Friendship. It cannot suppress Memories. It cannot silence Courage. It cannot invade the Soul. It cannot steal Eternal Life. It cannot conquer the Spirit. Cancer is so limited!"*

Cancer certainly can be a life-changing experience. It can change how we view ourselves, our future, and our view of life itself. It can change our daily life – perhaps for a few years, perhaps for the rest of our life. It may change the kind of work we do and our recreational choices. And, as is true for all long-term trials, cancer can change our relationships.

Through my own experiences and the pain and suffering I have witnessed in the lives of others, I have learned that WE NEED ONE ANOTHER. God never intended for us to go it alone. At the very beginning of the human race, God said, "It is not good for man to be alone." That is why I started my Reflections Ministry, focusing on endurance, perseverance, and positivity so that those struggling with Cancer and other life challenges will feel supported and not alone.

The connection between pain and spiritual strength is made repeatedly in Scripture. It is no accident, for example that the "wonder words" strong, firm, and steadfast in 1 Peter 5:10 appear in the context of "after you have suffered a little while." The young gymnasts referenced in this reflection have certainly demonstrated strong, firm, and steadfast endurance and perseverance in their quest for athletic success.

May we do the same in our quest for the "Eternal Gold" offered with our Lord and Savior Jesus Christ who gives us a chance at true life if we are only willing to be humble and learn His ways while we navigate the challenges that life "pitches" our way!

### An Encouraging Attitude:
"Cancer is so limited… It cannot cripple Love. It cannot shatter Hope. It cannot corrode Faith. It cannot destroy Peace. It cannot kill Friendship. It cannot suppress Memories. It cannot silence Courage. It cannot invade the Soul. It cannot steal Eternal Life. It cannot conquer the Spirit. Cancer is so limited!"

### *A Spiritual Insight:*

*"We can rejoice too, when we run into problems and trials, for we know that they help us develop endurance. And endurance develops strength of character, and character strengthens our confident hope of salvation. And this hope will not lead to disappointment." Romans 5:3-5 NLT*

### *A Step to Consider:*

The connection between pain and spiritual strength is made repeatedly in Scripture. It is no accident, for example that the "wonder words" strong, firm, and steadfast in 1 Peter 5:10 appear in the context of "after you have suffered a little while." The young gymnasts referenced in this reflection have certainly demonstrated strong, firm, and steadfast endurance and perseverance in their quest for athletic success.

# Reflection 42

## *"What Happens Next?"*

*August 24, 2024*

"*The future is not frightening if you know the future. And you can know the future when you know who holds it.*"

*Max Lucado* [46]

Not sure about you, but every time I violate my personal mental health prescription and turn on the news, I tend to be plunged into despair… When I survey today's social media, I too often see overwhelming fear, anger, gloom, and doom. I certainly understand the need to be informed, but I am beginning to think that fear is the most consistent ingredient for far too many sources these days.

I remember reading *Chicken Little* when I was a kid, and I have also read the story to my grandkids. The story tells about a young chick walking along who is unexpectedly struck on the head by an acorn. With no further investigation, Chicken Little (Henny Penny) came to the conclusion that so often permeates our social media today... THE SKY IS FALLING!

Today Chicken Little would be an excellent politician, or better yet, cable news anchor. The sky is falling! Look! There is an expert displaying a colorful chart to prove it! I understand the importance of communicating information for our awareness and safety, but the tone and volume of fear mongering these days is likely to send a person into a downward spiral!

So, how do I process this tsunami of doom? Personally, I need to remind myself of some of the fundamental truths that I hold true. I find myself doing this over and over because the noise from our current culture can often drown out the quiet voice of the Spirit of God.

These events are NOT a surprise to God. Violence, hatred, bigotry, and division are a product of a fallen world that will someday be redeemed. Jesus made it very clear that following Him is not a "get out of grief" card.

> *"I have told you all this so that you may have peace in me. Here on earth, you will have many trials and sorrows. But take heart, because I have overcome the world" (John 16:33, NLT).*

Yes, there will certainly be troubles, we have all experienced them! Health issues, relationship problems, financial concerns... But what does "He has overcome the world" mean? It means even in my deepest fear and darkest hour I know that I am loved, adopted, redeemed, and I have the promise of eternity with God. I have hope to sustain me. I am not anxious to leave this world, but I am also not afraid. I believe I have an eternal inheritance given as a free gift of grace awaiting me.

I try my best to follow the laws and guidelines society lays out for me. I try to be a good neighbor and a responsible citizen. After doing those things, I believe I have come to the conclusion drawn by David when he was afraid for his future. His lament sounds like he could have written it today—after watching cable news of course!

> *"My heart is breaking as I remember how it used to be: I walked among the crowds of worshipers, leading a great procession to the house of God, singing for joy and giving thanks amid the sound of a great celebration!" Psalm 42:4-6 NLT*

David was isolated. His days of joyful gatherings were just a memory as he hunkered down alone in fear. But he remembered the key to his joy and thankfulness. He remembered where he placed his hope.

*"Why am I discouraged? Why is my heart so sad? I will put my hope in God! I will praise him again–my Savior and my God!" Psalm 42:5-6 NLT*

The next time the news or a social media influencer is causing your heart to be downcast, I'd encourage you to remember the words of Paul to the church at Corinth.

*"For our present troubles are small and won't last very long. Yet they produce for us a glory that vastly outweighs them and will last forever! So, we don't look at the troubles we can see now; rather, we fix our gaze on things that cannot be seen. For the things we see now will soon be gone, but the things we cannot see will last forever" (2 Corinthians 4:17-18, NLT).*

I am working at choosing to focus my gaze, whenever I can, on the source of our hope and light as followers of Jesus. Fear often causes us to take our eye off the source of our strength. If we keep our eyes on Jesus, it will help us get through the unpleasing atmosphere of doom and gloom that too often surrounds us.

More than a few "end of times" dates have come and passed, which are often accompanied by a great deal of fear. I have been reading a recent release by one of my favorite authors, Max Lucado. In his book, *What Happens Next,* Max helps take the fear out of the craziness that surrounds us in today's culture.

In contrast to the confusion and anxiety that often comes with this topic, Max Lucado believes God wants us to be prepared, not scared; informed, not intimidated. He writes: "The future is not frightening if you know the future. And you can know the future when you know who holds it."

Whether you find yourself in the "I can't wait," "I'm almost ready," or "I'm not sure about all of this" camp, you will be encouraged to ponder God's promises for the future in his book. And, in his signature and encouraging style, Max reminds us, "It's all about hope. It's all about Him."

### *An Encouraging Attitude:*
"The future is not frightening if you know the future. And you can know the future when you know who holds it." Max Lucado

### *A Spiritual Insight:*
*"For our present troubles are small and won't last very long. Yet they produce for us a glory that vastly outweighs them and will last forever! So, we don't look at the troubles we can see now; rather, we fix our gaze on things that cannot be seen. For the things we see now will soon be gone, but the things we cannot see will last forever" (2 Corinthians 4:17-18, NLT).*

### *A Step to Consider:*

Whether you find yourself in the "I can't wait," "I'm almost ready," or "I'm not sure about all of this" camp, you will be encouraged to ponder God's promises for the future if we remember "It's all about hope. It's all about Him."

# Reflection 43

# *"Fighting One More Round?"*

*September 1, 2024*

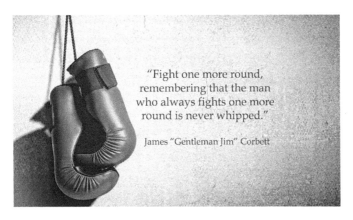

"Fight one more round, remembering that the man who always fights one more round is never whipped."

James "Gentleman Jim" Corbett

*"You become a champion by fighting one more round. When things are tough, you fight one more round remembering that the man who fights one more round is never whipped."*
**James J. Corbett**

So many of us battle something that tends to recur in our lives and when it does the frustration can be intensely frustrating. *"I should be better than this. Why can't I get past this? Why do I continue to do this?"* At times like that it's worth remembering that if we get frustrated with ourselves, things compound, and we end up in a spiral. I've come to the realization that getting frustrated certainly doesn't help me improve.

However, taking a breath and getting back to work will. Understanding that the thoughts we are having at the moment will pass and giving them a chance to do so will help us move on to something better. I have experienced those thoughts many times since being diagnosed. I've made a commitment not to give in to frustration or hopelessness, and to continue to face the challenges of a cancer journey with an attitude that I developed early on in my cancer journey. As Boxer James "Gentleman Jim" Corbett shared:

> *"You become a champion by fighting one more round. When things are tough, you fight one more round remembering that the man who fights one more round is never whipped." James J. Corbett* [47]

I recently lost a friend to cancer who had battled the disease for many years. Peggy Novak fought that battle with grace, humility, courage, and faith. She battled through the fear, pain, and agony that this journey brings and provided such positive inspiration to those who struggle on their personal journeys with cancer. Peggy kept Jesus at her side the entire way and her faith in Him supplied her the strength and courage needed to complete her journey here on earth. She truly was an inspirational example of continuing to "fight one more round", and knowing she is now pain free in Heaven with Jesus means cancer never "whipped her"!

Fear is certainly an overwhelming emotion that can take hold of us, sometimes causing complete irrationality. Sometimes fear can even be more devastating than the very thing we are afraid of, even with a "fighting attitude" firmly in place. But God says that as followers of Jesus Christ, we don't have to be afraid. Why? Because He is with us.

*"He will cover you with his feathers. He will shelter you with his wings. His faithful promises are your armor and protection" (Psalm 91:4 NLT).*

I think we must also be aware that what the psalmist isn't saying is that God's people will be immune to difficulties in life. There are Christians who have faced calamities and hardships. And there are Christians who have been victims of crimes. Therefore, these verses don't give us a carte blanche promise that we never will face any difficulty. Instead, they give us a promise from God that He will be with us, no matter what we go through. And He will see us through.

God has a work He is going to do in each our lives. I've often said, "God didn't save me from something, but rather for something." I've felt God has asked that I do my best to not only promote positivity and encouragement for those on a similar journey, but also to continue to remind others that God is always with us on our personal journeys. And until He is done with that work each of us are intended for according to His plan, we are indestructible.

We see this illustrated in the story of the apostle Paul after he was shipwrecked. As Paul attended to a fire, a poisonous snake bit his hand. But Paul simply shook off the snake into the fire. Paul wasn't affected by the venom because God wasn't finished with Paul yet.

In the same way, God will keep us on earth and be with us here until He has completed His work through our lives. I haven't been bitten by any poisonous snakes lately... but given the current state of craziness in our world, there are so many things today that can strike fear in our hearts. Yet as we look at a frightening world, we can have courage, not because of who we are but because God is with us. His presence in our lives can help us be fearless in a frightening world!

*"Consider it pure joy, my brothers, whenever you
face trials of many kinds, because you know that
the testing of your faith develops perseverance."
James 1:2-3*

There is no joy in the trial, but there is joy in the knowledge of how God uses such events in our lives. If you are in the midst of a trial or about to face a trial, take comfort that God desires for you to emerge strengthened and beautiful and useful. An excerpt from *Stay: Lessons My Dogs Taught Me About Life, Loss and Grace* by Dave Burchett speaks to my heart...

> "One potter said that the greatest thing about making pots is that each lump of clay has near-infinite potential. The lump of clay that is me and the lump of clay that is you have infinite potential because we have an infinite God who is patient and good. We should not fear or run from fiery trials. What happens when we endure them while trusting God is worth the cost." [48]

Let's continue to face life's challenges by always being willing to "fight one more round when things get tough" while remembering that God is always in our corner ready to help attend to those cuts, bumps and bruises we acquire along the way!

### An Encouraging Attitude:

"You become a champion by fighting one more round. When things are tough, you fight one more round remembering that the man who fights one more round is never whipped." James J. Corbett

### A Spiritual Insight:

*"Consider it pure joy, my brothers, whenever you face trials of many kinds, because you know that the testing of your faith develops perseverance." James 1:2-3*

### A Step to Consider:

Let's continue to face life's challenges by always being willing to "fight one more round when things get tough" while remembering that God is always in our corner ready to help attend to those cuts, bumps and bruises we acquire along the way!

# Reflection 44

# *"Coincidence Is God's Way of Remaining Anonymous"*

*September 20, 2024*

If you lived my life, you wouldn't believe in coincidence. I shouldn't even be here.

Catherine DePasquale

*When you enter someone's life, whether by plan, chance, or coincidence, consider what your lesson will be. Will you teach love or a harsh lesson of reality?*

*Clint Hurdle*

I have spent some time recently reflecting on the concept of having more loving, less hurting, more comfort and less pain in our lives given all the negativity and hurting happening in our world today. As I'm getting older, my next birthday will require room for a bit more than 70 candles, so I'll most likely need a fire extinguisher to blow them all out! My hair is grayer, and my hourglass has much more sand on the bottom than on the top...

Given all that, I'm not only concerned about the present, but I'm also curious about the future. Those issues are certainly not new in this world of ours, but a recent devotion shared by one of my favorite baseball personalities, Clint Hurdle, shares some Godly advice that I think would benefit us all.

The Devotion simply speaks for itself...

Clint Hurdle writes:

*A ninety-one-year-old woman died after living a long-dignified life. When she met God, she asked him something that had long bothered her.*

*"If humans are created in God's image, and if all humans are created equal, why do people treat each other so badly?"*

*God replied that each person who enters our life has a unique lesson to teach us. And it is only through these lessons that we learn about life, people, relationships, and God. This confused the woman, so God began to explain:*

*When someone lies to you, it teaches you that things are not always as they seem. The truth is often far beneath the surface. Look beyond the masks people wear if you want to know their heart. And remove your own masks to let people know yours.*

*When someone steals from you, it teaches you that nothing is forever. Always appreciate what you have, for you never know when you might lose it. And never, ever take your friends and family for granted because today is the only guarantee you have.*

*When someone inflicts an injury upon you, it teaches you that the human state is a fragile one. Protect and take care of your body as best you can; it's the only thing you are sure to have forever.*

*When someone mocks you, it teaches you that no two people are alike. When you encounter people who are different from you, don't judge them by how they look or act; instead base your opinion on the contents of their heart.*

When someone breaks your heart, it teaches you that loving someone does not always mean that person will love you back. But don't turn your back on love, because when you find the right person, the joy that one person brings will make up for all the past hurts put together. Times ten.

When someone holds a grudge against you, it teaches you that everyone makes mistakes. When you are wronged, the most virtuous thing you can do is forgive the offender without pretense. Forgiving those who have hurt us is the most difficult and courageous thing a person can do.

When a loved one is unfaithful to you, it teaches you that resisting temptation is one's greatest challenge. Be vigilant in your resistance against all temptation. By doing so, you will be rewarded with an enduring sense of satisfaction far greater than the temporary pleasure by which you were tempted.

When someone cheats you, it teaches you that greed is the root of all evil. Aspire to make your dreams come true, no matter how lofty they may be. Do not feel guilty about your success, but never let an obsession with achieving your goals lead you to engage in malevolent activities.

When someone ridicules you, it teaches you that nobody is perfect. Accept people for their merits and be tolerant of their flaws. Do not ever reject someone for imperfections over which they have no control.

Upon hearing the Lord's wisdom, the old woman became concerned that there were no lessons to be learned from human's good deeds.

God replied that human's capacity to love is the greatest gift the human has. At the root of all kindness is love, and each act of love also teaches us a lesson.

The woman's curiosity deepening, God once again began to explain.

When someone loves us, it teaches us that love, kindness, charity, honesty, humility, forgiveness, and acceptance can counteract all the evil in the world. For every good deed, there

269

*is one less evil deed. A human alone has the power to control the balance between good and evil, but because the lessons of love are not taught often enough, the power is too often abused.*

*Here's some Godly advice:*

*When you enter someone's life, whether by plan, chance, or coincidence, consider what your lesson will be. Will you teach love or a harsh lesson of reality?*

*When you die, will your life have resulted in more loving or hurting? More comfort or pain? More joy or sadness?*

*Each one of us has power over the balance of love in the world. Use it wisely.*

*Make a difference today,*
*Love Clint* [49]

Some wonderful advice as we each get closer to *Nearing Home* on our life's journey! Each one of us truly does have some power over the balance of love in this world, so we do need to use it wisely.

As we travel the path of our remaining time here on this earth, let's focus on spreading more loving than hurting, more comfort than pain, and more joy than sadness. By choosing God as our partner the rest of the way, the future empowers us to face the present. Paul makes that clear in Philippians when he says...

> *"Brothers and sisters, I do not consider myself yet to have taken hold of it. But one thing I do: Forgetting what is behind and straining toward what is ahead, I press on toward the goal to win the prize for which God has called me heavenward in Christ Jesus." Philippians 3:13-14*

It is not by coincidence that each of us can help make those differences! As Catherine Delasquale shares, "If you've lived my life, you wouldn't believe in coincidence. I shouldn't even be here." Wow, does that ring a bell for me!

God often works behind the scenes to help us achieve the goal of spreading the values of love, comfort, and joy. I have witnessed this many times in my life journey as others have come into my life, sometimes as complete strangers, to help encourage me with positivity when I needed it most. Albert Einstein may have said it best in his book titled *The World As I See It*.

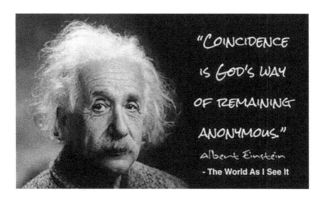

"Coincidence is God's Way of Remaining Anonymous" [50]

May each of us use those "coincidences" to bring about the positivity and encouragement needed to increase the LOVE we can experience in this world by spreading more loving than hurting, more comfort than pain, and more joy than sadness.

As I think through Reflection 44, I also find it interesting that the symbolic interpretations of the number 44 in Christianity are diverse and varied. They highlight its connection to transformation, spiritual growth, and faith, providing us with spiritual insights that can help us navigate our way through life with greater wisdom and understanding. Coincidence? Maybe... My hope is that this series of Reflections can help provide those insights as we each get closer to Nearing Home!

## *An Encouraging Attitude:*
God often works behind the scenes to help us achieve the goal of spreading the values of love, comfort, and joy. "Coincidence is God's Way of Remaining Anonymous" Albert Einstein

## *A Spiritual Insight:*
*"Brothers and sisters, I do not consider myself yet to have taken hold of it. But one thing I do: Forgetting what is behind and straining toward what is ahead, I press on toward the goal to win the prize for which God has called me heavenward in Christ Jesus." Philippians 3:13-14*

## *A Step to Consider:*
May each of us use those "coincidences" to bring about the positivity and encouragement needed to increase the LOVE we can experience in this world by spreading more loving than hurting, more comfort than pain, and more joy than sadness.

# Reflection 45

# *"Preparing for the Post Season"*

"God always has a plan and having faith in that plan will never fail you"!..Dansby Swanson

One of my goals as a coach was to always review with my players a fundamentals checklist as the regular season ended each year. The checklist was intended to highlight a series of specific fundamentals we had learned from instruction and experiences during the regular season. It provided a take-away for my players to carry with them into tournament play, with a goal of helping us to be successful as we played into the post season. Just as this checklist was helpful to my teams, I wanted to provide readers with a "post-season" checklist from these reflections as you, a family member or friend travel their life's journey facing the challenges life may present.

The following checklist of encouraging attitudes, spiritual insights, and steps to consider have helped provide me with some basic "fundamentals" which I have found to be useful throughout my life experience and as I continue my post-season journey as a cancer survivor. May they do the same for you and those you love as you step closer to "Nearing Home" on your life's journey!

# *Summary of Encouraging Attitudes, Spiritual Insights and Steps to Consider*

## *Reflection 1 – Seeking Wisdom in our Lives...*

### *An Encouraging Attitude:*
"The purpose of hospitality is to provide an environment and space where relationships can be nurtured and can grow without distraction. May we come to know that true hospitality is achieved not only when we share our things, but each other." Pastor Brian King, Nazareth Lutheran Church

### *A Spiritual Insight:*
*"We put our hope in the Lord. He is our help and our shield." Psalm 33:20*

### *A Step to Consider:*
As we move forward on our life journeys, whatever direction that may take each of us, sharing a hospitable space with others as we share our beliefs and opinions, while focusing on God's word, Jesus's love and depending on the Holy Spirit's guidance, we can make a positive impact and truly make a difference in our world... Let the journey continue!

# Reflection 2 – Give Each Day a Chance

### An Encouraging Attitude:
"All she asked was for me to give each day a chance. If a bad day comes along, just battle the day. A bad day lasts only 24 hours. If you can get through that bad one, a good day might follow. Take each day one at a time. Then leave it for what it is." Sparky Anderson

### A Spiritual Insight:
*"Do not despise these small beginnings, for the Lord rejoices to see the work begin." (Zech. 4:10).*

### A Step to Consider:
Please help us to begin… Just BEGIN! What seems small to each of us might be huge to someone else!! Things may not always go our way, or we might not feel well, *but together, with YOU* we can find a way to battle through it with tomorrow being a fresh start offering us some HOPE taking one day at a time.

# Reflection 3 – "Beautifully Broken…"

### An Encouraging Attitude:
May we all be kind and offer encouragement to those in our lives who may be experiencing brokenness on their life journey.

### A Spiritual Insight:
*The LORD is close to the brokenhearted; He rescues those who are crushed in spirit. Psalm 34:18*

### A Step to Consider:
There are so many brokenhearted people who simply need a caring heart. I know my *"Home Team"* has so often been there for me through my difficult times when my heart has been

heavy. We often tend to condemn those who may appear broken hearted not really knowing the reason they may be struggling through life's problems and heartaches.

In the Gospel of John, Jesus talked about the Holy Spirit coming to be our advocate and comforter on this earth. He left this amazing promise that I cling to more fervently every day. "I am leaving you with a gift—peace of mind and heart. And the peace I give is a gift the world cannot give. So don't be troubled or afraid." John 14:27

## Reflection 4–"Help Ohers, Even When They Can't Help Back!"

### An Encouraging Attitude:
Throughout Scripture, God promises us that he is with us — we do not have to be afraid or feel hopeless.

### A Spiritual Insight:
*"So do not fear, for I am with you; do not be dismayed, for I am your God. I will strengthen you and help you; I will uphold you with my righteous right hand" Isaiah 41:10.*

### A Step to Consider:
We have a chance daily to make others feel welcomed and loved. We have an opportunity to remind them that they matter and that their life is a gift. It might, in fact, be the most important thing they learn this school year! Don't miss the chance to teach it to them today. Today is your day. Live inspired... and maybe, just maybe, that is your purpose!

# Reflection 5 – *"When Life Gets Blurry, Adjust Your Focus!"*

### An Encouraging Attitude:
Heat, pressure, disappointment, and constraints may add up to create a wonderful outcome in our lives as we face the challenges that may come our way. For each of us, the heat, pressure, disappointment, and constraints may take on a different look. But take comfort. The heat and pressure may be pulling things (juices) out of you that you do not even realize. You just may even become a more tender (compassionate) and inviting person.

### A Spiritual Insight:
*"In his name (Jesus) the nations will put their hope."*
*Matthew 12:21*

### A Step to Consider:
Each of us have goals and things we want to accomplish, and maybe the road to get there looks just as daunting (or even more so) than a seven-month baseball season. I have discovered that my best chance for success lies in taking steps, no matter how small, towards that goal each day.

# Reflection 6 – *"Be an Encourager!"*

### An Encouraging Attitude:
As a cancer survivor, I have done my best to continue sharing encouragement, inspiration and support for others who may be facing not only serious health issues such as cancer, but other life challenges as well since my cancer diagnosis in 2009. Please consider being an encourager by donating to te American Cancer Society.

*A Spiritual Insight:*
*"Each of us should please our neighbors for their good, to build them up. Romans 15:2*

*A Step to Consider:*
The game of baseball provides many lessons about success and failure, and those lessons can often be applied in our life journeys. As life's curveballs and challenges come our way, I encourage reaching out to your "Home Teams" (both human and divine) for the strength, love, support, and comfort needed to meet them.

## *Reflection 7–"Extinguish the 'Thought Bubbles' of the Past!"*

*An Encouraging Attitude:*
Can you spare a few minutes (in the present) to send a text/ email, or even better, a quick phone call? It will make a huge difference in their day and take just a small investment of time from you. An investment that will surely pay dividends when you realize how much it meant to them. Moving forward, work at simply picking out just one person in your life to reach out to each day and encourage them. It will surely have a positive impact on them.

*A Spiritual Insight:*
*"Therefore, do not worry about tomorrow, for tomorrow will worry about itself. Each day has enough trouble of its own."*
*Matthew 6:34*

*A Step to Consider:*
I've found it helpful to be aware of just how often I'm not living in the present in my life. When I catch myself worrying

about the future, or cursing the past, I gently remind myself to get back to the present and the task that is right in front of me.

## Reflection 8 – "If You're Happy and You Know It Tell Your Face!"

### An Encouraging Attitude:
We are uniquely and completely designed for our role in this world, let's approach it with a smile. So, let's all join in that familiar Sunday School song...If you're happy and you know it, Tell your face. If you're happy and you know it, Tell your face. If you're happy and you know it, Then your face should really show it. If you're happy and you know it Tell your face!

### A Spiritual Insight:
*"A glad heart makes a happy face; a broken heart crushes the spirit." Proverbs 15:13*

### A Step to Consider:
"You were born an original. Don't die a copy."

## Reflection # 9 – "What is the Tie That Will Unite Us as Christians?"

### An Encouraging Attitude:
Our life journeys are full of frustrating situations and frustrating people. But I believe with all my heart that there are sacred moments to be found in even the most mundane of days. Whether I acknowledge it or not, God is the middle of everything I do. This week's mental post-note is very simple...*Today Is Sacred*.

279

### *A Spiritual Insight:*
"Search me, O God, and know my heart, test me, and know my anxious thoughts. Point out anything in me that offends you and lead me along the path of everlasting life. (Psalm 139:23-24, NLT)

### *A Step to Consider:*
I try to remind myself that through God's Spirit today and every day is sacred. Let us use that spirit as an instrument to show our love and grace to each other every day. And when we feel emotions, don't fight them, let them wash over us and pass. They are only temporary. Just like in life, we can't force things, but we can find a way to move forward together using Christ as our ultimate and divine tie... It might even include being kind to unkind people because they need it the most!!

## *Reflection # 10 – "Never Forget Who That One Person May Be in Your Life!"*

### *An Encouraging Attitude:*
"Don't walk behind me; I may not lead. Don't walk in front of me; I may not follow. Just walk beside me and be my friend."
Albert Camus

### *A Spiritual Insight:*
"It is not the healthy who need a doctor but the sick." Luke 5:31

### *A Step to Consider:*
Let's keep in mind that it is the hearts that we touch and the lives we enrich that will be our deepest and most meaningful legacy. The most important thing in life is people, not things.

# Reflection # 11 – "Looking UP to Where Our Help Comes From..."

### An Encouraging Attitude:
Because life's uncertainties seem on the increase, where can we find hope when what we've hoped for and planned seems to be passing away? As Christians, we can turn to God, who is unshakable, unmovable, and everlasting, in whom we can put our future hope and trust in without fear.

### A Spiritual Insight:
*"The Lord will keep you from all harm—he will watch over your life; the Lord will watch over your coming and going both now and forevermore." Psalm 121:7-8*

### A Step to Consider:
Let's leave our pessimism at the door while embracing the "old grumpy man" in ourselves as we move forward in loving and caring community. Together, while trusting our Father's faithfulness, we can look to the future with positivity and hope as we delight in each other's company making it a priority that no one ever feels alone.

# Reflection # 12 – "Leadership is a Life of Service"

### An Encouraging Attitude:
The message I want to share with today's post is twofold... First, we need to accept each other despite our differences or disabilities, just a Christ accepts each of us... Secondly, just as George Springer reached out to Mateo, leading with his friendship and support while providing the inspiration and motivation for Mateo to help overcome his disability, may each of us use every opportunity we are granted to become servant leaders and do the same.

### A Spiritual Insight:
*"Not so with you. Instead, whoever wants to become great among you must be your servant." Matthew 20:26*

### A Step to Consider:
Jesus taught His disciples that servant leadership was the pre-scribed form of leadership for the Kingdom of God. Then he modeled it! He modeled it by loving them. He modeled it by teaching them, by being patient with them, by washing their feet, and ultimately by going to the cross for them and for us.

## Reflection # 13 – "Every Day Can Be Like Opening Day!"

### An Encouraging Attitude:
I can believe that hope for the future is real. I can understand that I must be a better teammate to others that I encounter and not expect my team to be perfect. The magic of a fresh start happens once a year in baseball. It can happen any day and every day for a follower of Jesus.

### A Spiritual Insight:
*"If your gift is serving others, serve them well.*
*If you are a teacher, teach well.*
*If your gift is to encourage others, be encouraging.*
*If it is giving, give generously.*
*If God has given you leadership ability, take the responsibility seriously.*
*And if you have a gift for showing kindness to others, do it gladly.*
*Don't just pretend to love others. Really love them.*
*Hate what is wrong. Hold tightly to what is good.*
*Love each other with genuine affection and take delight in hon-oring each other.*
*Never be lazy but work hard and serve the Lord enthusiastically.*

*Rejoice in our confident hope. Be patient in trouble and keep on praying.*

*When God's people are in need, be ready to help them. Always be eager to practice hospitality.*

*Bless those who persecute you. Don't curse them; pray that God will bless them.*

*Be happy with those who are happy, and weep with those who weep. Live in harmony with each other. Don't be too proud to enjoy the company of ordinary people. And don't think you know it all! Never pay back evil with more evil. Do things in such a way that everyone can see you are honorable."*

*Romans 12: 7-17 NLT*

### A Step to Consider:

You are never too far gone for Jesus. Every single church is full of humans who are flawed but faithful, broken but believing, imperfect but inspired. People who may be hanging on by a thread, but grace keeps them hanging in there. So, if you are still thinking about it—just go. You will be welcomed. By the people. But most importantly, by Jesus."

# Reflection # 14 – "Listen, and Honor Other's Stories…!"

### An Encouraging Attitude:

I have listened to many stories on my cancer journey and now have a much better understanding of why people tend to react the way they do. And listening (really listening) can open a door to dialogue about your own journey and story. You will be acting as a true child of God by having that conversation!

### A Spiritual Insight:

*"You have heard the law that says, 'Love your neighbor' and hate your enemy. But I say, love your enemies! Pray for those*

*who persecute you! In that way, you will be acting as true children of your Father in heaven. For he gives his sunlight to both the evil and the good, and he sends rain on the just and the unjust alike. If you love only those who love you, what reward is there for that? Even corrupt tax collectors do that much. If you are kind only to your friends, how are you different from anyone else? Even unbelievers do that." Matthew 5:43-47, NLT*

### A Step to Consider:
If the message had been clean up your life and then you can be part of our community, the revival would have stopped cold. Instead, the message was come to know Jesus and let Him show you how to change how you live. That happened millions of times during that remarkable revival. It can still happen today. But my concern is that God cannot use us if we are busy broadbrushing everyone we disagree with. I want to share His story without judging theirs, so I am throwing away the broad-brush! May we all consider doing the same.

## Reflection # 15 – "If You Don't Have Hope, You Don't Have Anything."

### An Encouraging Attitude:
Just as Coach Wafula has inspired Kasumba to work hard at overcoming his circumstances while pursuing his dream, we need to remind ourselves that even though difficulties and challenges abound in this world, we can rejoice that Jesus is always present to help us cope with any and all circumstances, knowing that all things are possible with him.

### A Spiritual Insight:
*Jesus looked at them and said, "With man this is impossible, but not with God: all things are possible with God." Mark 10:27*

### A Step to Consider:

"My motto was always to keep swinging. Whether I was in a slump or feeling badly or having trouble off the field, the only thing to do was keep swinging." Hank Aaron

And that's what God wants us to do. Keep swinging. Don't be complacent. Don't get discouraged. Don't become cynical. There's a difference between knowing and doing. Keep swinging, and trust that the Holy Spirit will be working in and through you, despite your circumstances or perceived roadblocks.

## Reflection # 16 – "Life is About Adjustments!"

### An Encouraging Attitude:

My heartfelt thanks are extended to the American Cancer Society and the Black Hawk County Relay for Life for recognizing me as their 2023 Survivor of the year... Life most certainly is about adjustments, and, as one of my favorite coaches always told us; *"It's great to be alive!!"*

### A Spiritual Insight:

*"Be joyful in hope, patient in affliction, faithful in prayer."*
*Romans 12:12*

### A Step to Consider:

Making ourselves available to others can open the doors of opportunity for deeper relationships, healing, and transformation. For many, time is one of the most valuable commodities in today's fast-paced world. Sharing time with others is a wonderful gift. It says, "*Here I am... for you. To listen, to care, to serve.*" The power of presence should never be underestimated!

285

# *Reflection # 17 – "How Can We Stay Optimistic in a Pessimistic World?"*

### *An Encouraging Attitude:*
Something that gives me optimism in this fallen world is that I used to believe that my sin caused Jesus to leave my side until I repented and returned to His presence. Now I know He never leaves me in those moments. Through the presence of the Holy Spirit, I have the constant presence of God in my journey. I don't have to do anything except remember my need for forgiveness, grace, and love and turn to His constant presence. He is there always. Ready to encourage, love, and direct my path."
Dave Burchett

### *A Spiritual Insight:*
· *"I have said these things to you, that in me you may have peace. In the world you will have tribulation...But take heart; I have overcome the world." (John 16:33, NLT)*

### *A Step to Consider:*
May we all face the life challenges that come our way by remembering that every step we take with Jesus at our side brings us hope, knowing full well that He Lives!

# *Reflection # 18 – "Running A Relay For Life!"*

### *An Encouraging Attitude:*
"Because no matter what our experience with cancer has been, we all share the hope that we will one day live in a world where our children and their children will never have to hear the words 'you have cancer.'"

*A Spiritual Insight:*
*"Be joyful in hope, patient in affliction, faithful in prayer*
*"Romans 12:12*

*A Step to Consider:*
This is a time for us to grieve those we've lost and a time to reflect on how the disease has touched each of us personally. It's a time to look inside ourselves with quiet reflection and find home. At our Relay for Life, we share moments of laughter, moments of silence, provide shoulders to cry on or hands to high-five, and we raise funds to help the American Cancer Society develop breakthrough research, provide free lodging to patients, and give free rides for treatment.

# *Reflection # 19 – "Who Is Your Favorite Superhero?"*

*An Encouraging Attitude:*
Some days we may feel like Clark Kent. But it's time to remember this truth: you can be Superman/Superwoman too, and the best is yet to come with Jesus at our side!

*A Spiritual Insight:*
*"Come to me, all of you who are weary and carry heavy burdens, and I will give you rest. Take my yoke upon you. Let me teach you, because I am humble and gentle at heart, and you will find rest for your souls. For my yoke is easy to bear, and the burden I give you is light." (Matthew 11:28-30)*

*A Step to Consider:*
I know who I have turned to when I need some time to retreat and refresh... I often write about the importance of Christian community, and it is there where I have so often found peace

287

and comfort during my times of challenge. Some real-life Superheroes truly do exist there!

## *Reflection # 20 – "Don't Argue With Reality!"*

### *An Encouraging Attitude:*
As Byron Katie says. "When you argue with reality, you lose, but only 100% of the time." If baseball has taught me anything over the years, it is a common fact that you will not win an argument with the umpire, the "ultimate authority" in a game... believe me, I've tried on occasion.)

### *A Spiritual Insight:*
*"So now I am giving you a new commandment: Love each other. Just as I have loved you, you should love each other."* *John 15:12*

### *A Step to Consider:*
...So that is my agenda. To love others as I have been loved and to be a support and helpful servant to those who may be struggling with hope in the "reality" of their life journey.

## *Reflection # 21 – "Fundamentals... Getting Back to Basics!"*

### *An Encouraging Attitude:*
Of course, a loving, caring and supportive community isn't the only ingredient for success, but it's certainly a key ingredient that helps make us, everything we do and everyone around us better. Just as in football, when we learn the fundamentals, the rest of the offense falls into place.

*A Spiritual Insight:*
*"Dear brothers and sisters, if another believer is overcome by some sin, you who are godly should gently and humbly help that person back onto the right path. And be careful not to fall into the same temptation yourself. Share each other's burdens, and in this way obey the law of Christ. If you think you are too important to help someone, you are only fooling yourself. You are not that important." (Galatians 6:1-3)*

*A Step to Consider:*
Just a reminder that as we get back to the basics, remember He is our Father who loves us and wants the best for us. If the answer is no that is an answer. That may mean our request may be answered later, or it may be answered differently. It may not even be answered at all. But through all those responses we must trust that He is holy, powerful, and present. Let's all embrace that fundamental truth as we continue our life journeys.

## Reflection # 22 – "Hard Things Put in Our Way Call for Courage!"

*An Encouraging Attitude:*
Rickey's story illustrates for me that the human spirit is one of ability, perseverance, and courage that no disability can steal away! It proves that hard things are put in our way, not to stop us, but to call out our courage and strength.

*A Spiritual Insight:*
*"Trust in the Lord with all your heart; do not depend on your own understanding. Seek his will in all you do, and he will show you which path to take." Proverbs 3:5-6*

**A Step to Consider:**
"Start by doing what's necessary, then do what's possible, and suddenly you are doing the impossible." St Francis of Assisi

## *Reflection # 23 – "An Unspoken Bond"*

**An Encouraging Attitude:**
*"OUR FRIENDSHIP TRANSCENDS TYPICAL SPEECH. THIS FRIENDSHIP IS ESPECIALLY IMPORTANT BECAUSE IT GIVES ME FAITH THAT MY TRUE SELF IS VALUED IN SPITE OF MY UNRULY BODY." Reece Blankenship*

**A Spiritual Insight:**
*Jesus showed we need to show kindness and compassion to not only the neighbors we are comfortable with, but especially to those we are uncomfortable with. We cannot look away when we encounter any person in need no matter what their color, status, beliefs, disabilities, or behaviors might be. We are called to compassion, and only that kind of faith will cause change. Theme of Luke 10:29-37*

**A Step to Consider:**
"If I can help someone, I don't need to think or pray about it. I just do it."

## *Reflection # 24 – "Heaven has Gained Another Angel!"*

**An Encouraging Attitude:**
I've realized over time that every time it rains, it stops raining. Every time you hurt; you heal. After darkness always comes light and I will be reminded of this each and every time my

special memories of mom fill my heart and my mind. She will always be a part of who I am.

**A Spiritual Insight:**
" *Charm is deceptive, and beauty does not last; but a woman who fears the LORD will be greatly praised." Proverbs 31:30*

**A Step to Consider:**
In that moment I realized that I have been on the receiving end of more love from her than most receive in a lifetime. I had no more troubling thoughts about her death at that point. My mom was at peace, and one day I will know that peace too. One day we'll all be in our heavenly home, together again with mom, who gave my earthly home such meaning.

## Reflection # 25 – *"Finding Hope and Restoration…"*

**An Encouraging Attitude:**
God has a plan and a purpose for each of us, but to know the will of God, we must surrender our hearts to Him.

**A Spiritual Insight:**
*"I no longer call you slaves because a master doesn't confide in his slaves. Now you are my friends, since I have told you every-thing the Father told me" (John 15:15 NLT).*

**A Step to Consider:**
When we put our faith in Jesus Christ, we begin a special friendship with God. God has given us a user's manual in life called the Bible, which helps us to understand the will of God. God is essentially saying, "Give Me your life, and I will show you My will." The condition of an enlightened mind is a sur-rendered heart…

## *Reflection # 26 – "Showing Love Through Our Actions!"*

### *An Encouraging Attitude:*
When the Lord told His followers that they're to love the way He does, He wasn't talking about what we find in popular culture. Jesus gave them the ultimate image of self-sacrificing love: a person laying down his life for a friend (John 15:13).

### *A Spiritual Insight:*
*"Let each of you look not only to his own interests, but also to the interests of others. (Philippians 2:4)*

### *A Step to Consider:*
Christians should be looking for ways to show love through our actions. Our thoughts and prayers need hands and feet displaying the love of Christ to have eternal impact. It is hard to spend much time in the New Testament and not realize the challenge for Christians toward those hurting, in need, and devoid of hope.

## *Reflection # 27 – "Finding Hope in Hurt..."*

### *An Encouraging Attitude:*
We can all find Hope in the Hurt! Whatever hardships we may be walking through, we must have hope and trust that God is painting a picture of wholeness and transformation, even if we can't see it, we need to look for beauty and goodness—it is there. I am trusting that promise for myself and my friends and family who may be hurting...

### *A Spiritual Insight:*
*"In his kindness God called you to share in his eternal glory by means of Christ Jesus. So, after you have suffered a little while,*

*He will restore, support, and strengthen you, and He will place you on a firm foundation." (1 Peter 5: 10)*

**A Step to Consider:**
When you have nowhere else to turn but to Christ you find out that you should have turned to Him first all along! Jesus knows the human condition. He has already been where we are. When the hurt and the Healer collide something amazing happens. The pain may not immediately go away, but peace and hope begin to slowly heal the pain.

## Reflection # 28– "Where God's Love is, there is no Fear"

**An Encouraging Attitude:**
Simply put... Make love your motivation to help eliminate the fear and anxiety that life challenges can bring on.

**A Spiritual Insight:**
*"Where God's love is, there is no fear, because God's perfect love drives out fear."* 1 John 4:18 (NCV)

**A Step to Consider:**
As we move forward into 2024, let's carry Mother Teresa's timeless wisdom as a torch lighting our path. In forgiving, being kind, staying honest, finding joy, doing good and giving our best, we not only elevate ourselves but empower those around us to learn more, do more and become who they were meant to be.

# Reflection # 29– "Conversation with a Complete Stranger"

### An Encouraging Attitude:
Our awards, trophies, diplomas, and job titles will fade. But striving to be first in love, showing up for others, and making our lives about something far bigger than ourselves will be remembered not only after our death, but will positively change the world while we are alive. Let's all strive to be first in that race!

### A Spiritual Insight:
*"God created human beings to work in the world, to help the world be productive and to care for it." (Gen 2:15).*

### A Step to Consider:
As followers of Jesus, we are tasked to join our Lord in his redemptive, restorative work. Just as Roberto Clemente was doing when he boarded that plane to help bring aid to his friends in Nicaragua, our work as followers of Jesus includes all that we do to bear witness to him, to make disciples, to seek his kingdom and to love our neighbors.

# Reflection # 30 – "WHOSE WE ARE and WHO WE ARE"

### An Encouraging Attitude:
Just maybe we can all pause for a bit this Super Bowl weekend to consider two things: *"WHOSE WE ARE and WHO WE ARE"*. We are children of God. A God who went to great lengths to love us even though we were unlovable. So, how would a child of God respond victoriously? We show love!

### A Spiritual Insight:
*"Dear friends, let us continue to love one another, for love comes from God. Anyone who loves is a child of God and knows God."* 1 John 4:7

### A Step to Consider:
What should encourage all of us, though, is how God is building a time for those who trust in Him and His Son where the snaps, holds and kicks of our lives will be right down the middle. We just have to put our trust in Christ and follow Him with all our hearts. He's promised to take care of the rest after that.

## Reflection # 31 – "Keep Me in Your Heart, I'll Stay There Forever!"

### An Encouraging Attitude:
"If ever a day comes where we can't be together, keep me in your heart, I'll stay there forever" Winnie the Pooh

### A Spiritual Insight:
*"Let love and faithfulness never leave you; bind them around your neck, write them on the tablet of your heart."* Proverbs 3:3

### A Step to Consider:
We are all taught to be strong, but sometimes the strongest thing we can do is accept help. We are all taught to be modest, but sometimes the best thing we can do when we receive a compliment is simply to say thank you. Give them the gift of the good feeling that comes from helping another person.

## Reflection # 32 – "Don't Let the Old Man In!"

### An Encouraging Attitude:
Clint Eastwood was about to celebrate his 88th birthday by going to film a new movie. Toby Keith was blown away and asked him "how do you do it, man?" Eastwood answered, "I just get up every morning and go out. And I don't let the old man in."

### A Spiritual Insight:
*"We know that our old man was crucified with him so that the body of sin would no longer dominate us, so that we would no longer be enslaved to sin. Romans (6:6 NET)*

### A Step to Consider:
The next time I face the anxieties that life may bring my way, I will face them with a positive attitude and won't "LET THE OLD MAN IN!"

## Reflection # 33 – "Be the Living Expression of God's Kindness!"

### An Encouraging Attitude:
Having Jesus in your heart can make kindness and smiles happen!

### A Spiritual Insight:
*"And now, dear brothers and sisters, one final thing. Fix your thoughts on what is true, and honorable, and right, and pure, and lovely, and admirable. Think about things that are excellent and worthy of praise. Keep putting into practice all you learned and received from me—everything you heard from me and saw me doing. Then the God of peace will be with you."*
(Philippians 4:8-9 NLT)

*A Step to Consider:*
"Let no one ever come to you without leaving better and happier. Be the living expression of God's kindness: kindness in your face, kindness in your eyes, kindness in your smile."
Mother Teresa

## Reflection # 34 – "Never Make Predictions, Especially About the Future"

### An Encouraging Attitude:
One of the most important things that winning teams understand is that every teammate brings strengths and weaknesses to the team. A great team celebrates the strengths of each player and works together to offset the weaknesses.

### A Spiritual Insight:
*"I appeal to you, dear brothers and sisters, by the authority of our Lord Jesus Christ, to live in harmony with each other. Let there be no divisions in the church. Rather, be of one mind, united in thought and purpose. "I Corinthians 1:10*

### A Step to Consider:
Let's all work to find a Church Community, wherever that may be, that will help support each other in this Great Commission.

## Reflection # 35 – "The Signs in Life that Bring us Hope"

### An Encouraging Attitude:
We have become new creations now and forever in Jesus. Doesn't that hope feel especially good this spring? On many days we may feel the struggle, but Jesus guarantees one day we will "bloom" for eternity.

*A Spiritual Insight:*
"Therefore, if anyone is in Christ, he is a new creation. The old has passed away; behold, the new has come." 2 Corinthians 5:17

*A Step to Consider:*
Nothing we do for the Lord is ever useless. Nothing! And even as we face the reality of a dangerous world, we know we have the twin promise of victory over sin and death through Jesus. So as spring continues, lets choose to marvel at the renewing of life and the hope that holds for all of us.

## Reflection # 36 – "Seeking the 'Touch of the Master'"

*An Encouraging Attitude:*
It struck me that Josie's reaction to my touch and mere presence was a wonderful illustration of how Jesus comforts (or desires to comfort) me when I face difficult times. When I (her master) touched Josie, she was comforted. Her pain was not gone. She was still a bit disoriented and unsure. Josie's circumstances hadn't really changed at all. But she knew that her master was there and that made it better.

*A Spiritual Insight:*
"I rejoice greatly in the Lord that at last you have renewed your concern for me. Indeed, you have been concerned, but you had no opportunity to show it. I am not saying this because I am in need, for I have learned to be content whatever the circumstances. I know what it is to be in need, and I know what it is to have plenty. I have learned the secret of being content in any and every situation, whether well fed or hungry, whether living in plenty or in want." (Philippians 4, The Message)

*A Step to Consider:*
"Too often we underestimate the power of a touch, a smile, a kind word, a listening ear, an honest compliment, or the smallest act of caring, all of which have the potential to turn a life around."

# Reflection # 37 – "Picking Up the Pieces"

*An Encouraging Attitude:*
This hurting world and country of ours needs hope, light, and grace. We need thoughtful listeners with a message of love. We need the positive message of the Good News. I hope to continue to bring some positivity with my thoughts as I feel quite comfortable that the negative side will be well represented by countless others.

*A Spiritual Insight:*
*"Your love for one another will prove to the world that you are my disciples." John 13:35*

*A Step to Consider:*
May we each become a person of light, love, charity, hope, courage, joy, mercy, grace, and compassion as we become what God intends us to be!

# Reflection # 38 – "Making a Difficult Challenge Productive"

*An Encouraging Attitude:*
Maintaining a positive mindset helped provide me with the strength, hope, and resilience I needed during those difficult times. It allowed me to focus on possibilities, maintain a sense of control, and foster and internalize the belief that I could

fight and win over this disease! Embracing positivity helped me reduce stress, anxiety, and depression, while promoting my overall emotional well-being. A bit of a stubborn attitude I developed over my athletic career about *Never Giving Up* also may have helped!

### A Spiritual Insight:
*"You are the light of the world—like a city on a hilltop that cannot be hidden. No one lights a lamp and then puts it under a basket. Instead, a lamp is placed on a stand, where it gives light to everyone in the house. In the same way, let your good deeds shine out for all to see, so that everyone will praise your heavenly Father." (Matthew 5:14-16)*

### A Step to Consider:
Let's remember where our light comes from and pray that we can be a light shining for others. Let your good deeds reflect the loving light of our Father. You might be amazed how much of a difference that can make!

## Reflection # 39 – "Real Friends Are a Treasure!"

### An Encouraging Attitude:
...All friends are a blessing. Real friends are a treasure, and those friends are good for the heart and soul!

### A Spiritual Insight:
*"So now I am giving you a new commandment: Love each other. Just as I have loved you, you should love each other."* John 13:34 *NLT*

### A Step to Consider:
When we honestly ask ourselves which person in our lives means the most to us, we often find that it is those who, instead

of giving much advice, solutions, or cures, have chosen rather to share our pain and touch our wounds with a gentle and tender hand. The friend who can be silent with us in a moment of despair or confusion, who can stay with us in an hour of grief and bereavement, who can tolerate not knowing, not healing and face with us the reality of our powerlessness, that is a friend who cares...

## Reflection # 40 – "The More Love You Give the More Love You Will Have"

### An Encouraging Attitude:
There is a well-known saying that states people may not remember for what you said or did, but they will always remember the way you made them feel... More than their accomplishments, people are truly remembered for their acts of kindness, expressions of gratitude, and unwavering attitude of thankfulness.

### A Spiritual Insight:
*I could have no greater joy than to hear that my children (and grandchildren) are following the truth. (3 John 3:4, NLT)*

### A Step to Consider:
"The greatest legacy one can pass on to one's children and grandchildren is not money or other material things accumulated in one's life, but rather a legacy of character and faith."

## Reflection # 41 – "Perseverance and Endurance"

### An Encouraging Attitude:
"Cancer is so limited ... It cannot cripple Love. It cannot shatter Hope. It cannot corrode Faith. It cannot destroy Peace. It cannot

kill Friendship. It cannot suppress Memories. It cannot silence Courage. It cannot invade the Soul. It cannot steal Eternal Life. It cannot conquer the Spirit. Cancer is so limited!" – Author Unknown

### A Spiritual Insight:

*"We can rejoice too, when we run into problems and trials, for we know that they help us develop endurance. And endurance develops strength of character, and character strengthens our confident hope of salvation. And this hope will not lead to disappointment." Romans 5:3-5 NLT*

### A Step to Consider:

The connection between pain and spiritual strength is made repeatedly in Scripture. It is no accident, for example that the "wonder words" strong, firm, and steadfast in 1 Peter 5:10 appear in the context of "after you have suffered a little while." The young gymnasts referenced in this reflection have certainly demonstrated strong, firm, and steadfast endurance and perseverance in their quest for athletic success.

## *Reflection # 42 – "What Happens Next?"*

### An Encouraging Attitude:

"The future is not frightening if you know the future. And you can know the future when you know who holds it." Max Lucado

### A Spiritual Insight:

*"For our present troubles are small and won't last very long. Yet they produce for us a glory that vastly outweighs them and will last forever! So, we don't look at the troubles we can see now; rather, we fix our gaze on things that cannot be seen. For the things we see now will soon be gone, but the things we cannot see will last forever." (2 Corinthians 4:17-18, NLT)*

*A Step to Consider:*
Whether you find yourself in the "I can't wait," "I'm almost ready," or "I'm not sure about all of this" camp, you will be encouraged to ponder God's promises for the future if we remember 'It's all about hope. It's all about Him.'

## Reflection # 43 – "Fighting One More Round"

*An Encouraging Attitude:*
"You become a champion by fighting one more round. When things are tough, you fight one more round remembering that the man who fights one more round is never whipped." James J. Corbett

*A Spiritual Insight:*
*"Consider it pure joy, my brothers, whenever you face trials of many kinds, because you know that the testing of your faith develops perseverance." James 1:2-3*

*A Step to Consider:*
Let's continue to face life's challenges by always being willing to "fight one more round when things get tough" while remembering that God is always in our corner ready to help attend to those cuts, bumps and bruises we acquire along the way!

## Reflection # 44 – "Coincidence is God's Way of Remining Anonymous"

*An Encouraging Attitude:*
God often works behind the scenes to help us achieve the goal of spreading the values of love, comfort, and joy. "Coincidence is God's Way of Remaining Anonymous" Albert Einstein

## A Spiritual Insight:

*"Brothers and sisters, I do not consider myself yet to have taken hold of it. But one thing I do: Forgetting what is behind and straining toward what is ahead, I press on toward the goal to win the prize for which God has called me heavenward in Christ Jesus." Philippians 3:13-14*

## A Step to Consider:

May each of us use those "coincidences" to bring about the positivity and encouragement needed to increase the LOVE we can experience in this world by spreading more loving than hurting, more comfort than pain, and more joy than sadness.

# *Reflection Image Bibliography*

Front Cover Image; shutteerstock.com–1944185056

Rear Cover Image; shutterstock.com–622-01283685en_ Masterfile.jpg

About the Author Image; Personal Photo

Reflection # 1; Site Credit - https://m.facebook. com/story.php/?story_fbid=315668505768729 0&id=333949379960886.

Reflection # 2; Site Credit–https://therapeeds.com/en/blogs/ for-therapists/knowing-is-the-beginning-of-hope October 11, 2019

Reflection # 3; Facebook Pin on Faith and Scripture, Site Credit–https://www.facebook.com/people/ Beautifully-Broken/100068067301498/

Reflection # 4; Site Credit–https://www.today.com/parents/ parents-are-taking-toy-story-back-school-photos-t162362

Reflection # 4A; Site Credit: https://www.reddit.com/r/ GetMotivated/comments/xraqbt/image_help_others_ even_when_you_know_they_cant/?rdt=44942

Reflection # 5; Site Credit–https://x.com/actionhappiness/ status/988528849863544838

Reflection 5A; Site Credit: https://www.linkedin.com/posts/ matt-tonoli-545373136_perspective-keepmovingfor- ward-activity-7127997319148441600-Vuxh/

Reflection # 6; Hope Lodge – Site Credit: https://www. facebook.com/photo/?fbid=848391987138719&set =pcb.848392197138698

Reflection # 6A; Personal Photo

Reflection # 7; Site Credit–https://knowyourmeme.com/memes/this-is-why-the-dog-is-happier/photos

Reflection # 8; Snoopy on X, Site Credit https://x.com/snoopyfacts/status/900350308085227522

Reflection # 8A; Kim Steadman, Site Credit–https://kim-steadman.com/if-youre-happy-know-tell-face/

Reflection # 9; Site Credit: https://www.pinterest.es/pin/399694535691650581/

Reflection # 9A; Site Credit; https://www.pictorem.com/358502/Straight%20Railroad%20Tracks%20at%20Dusk.html

Reflection # 10; Site Credit–https://maswriter.medium.com/weve-all-been-joseph-ossai-792eda463875

Reflection # 10A; Site Credit; https://x.com/NYSPTA/status/1019205354029309952

Reflection # 11; Site Credit – A Man Called Otto, https://www.google.com/url?sa=i&url=https%3A%2F%2Fwww.imdb.com%2Ftitle%2Ftt7405458%2F&psig=AOvVaw-2tWW8ch94gajp8balunYQ4&ust=1719257803706000&-source=images&cd=vfe&opi=89978449&ved=0CBEQ-jRxqFwoTCJDT7sq88oYDFQAAAAAdAAAAABAE

Reflection # 11A; A Man Called Otto, Movie; Site Credit – https://www.latimes.com/enter-tainment-arts/movies/story/2022-12-28/man-called-otto-tom-hanks-mariana-trevino-review

Reflection # 12; Site Credit – Sled dog leadership, https://www.google.com/url?sa=i&url=https%3A%2F%2Fwww.linkedin.com%2Fpulse%2Fwhy-sled-dog-team-driv-ing-analogy-leadership-teamwork-dr-lu-cille-flime&psig=AOvVaw1tgPulTZT1Ip0EgHO-3ZO_x&ust=1719262759603000&source=images&c-d=vfe&opi=89978449&ved=0CBEQjRxqFwoTCJiX_ZfP8oYDFQAAAAAdAAAAABAE

Reflection # 12A; Site Credit – George Springer and Mateo Sanchez, https://www.mlb.com/news/george-springer-helped-writer-son-with-stutter

Reflection #13; Photo Courtesy of Atlanta Braves Inc.

Reflection #13A; Site Credit–https://www.google.com/url?sa=i&url=https%3A%2F%2Fwww.homage.com%2Fproducts%2Fst-louis-cardinals-here-for-the-hot-dogs-1&psig=AOvVaw1zCUhwrAMDJQGHY_pbWn-tA&ust=1719327921653000&source=images&c-d=vfe&opi=89978449&ved=0CBEQjRxqFwoTCMjPx-uPB9IYDFQAAAAdAAAAABAE

Reflection # 14; Pinterest – Site Credit; https://www.pinterest.com/pin/489907265705774653/

Reflection # 14A; thelifeididn'tchoose; Site Credit – https://thelifeididntchoose.com/2018/08/09/why-we-have-to-tell-our-stories-why-we-need-someone-to-listen/.

Reflection # 15, 15A, 15B, 15C; Kasumba Dennis Story with Ben Verlander, Site Credit–https://www.foxsports.com/watch/play-65d895db4001544

Reflection # 16; Freepik, Site Credit; https://www.freepik.com/premium-ai-image/man-walks-in-to-large-labyrinth-searching-solution-difficult-prob-lem-ai_47866400.htm

Reflection # 16A; Yogi Berra, ArtsyQuotes, Site Credit; https://www.walmart.com/ip/ArtsyQuotes-15x18-White-Modern-Wood-Framed-Museum-Art-Print-Titled-Yogi-Berra-Quote-Ninety-Percent-Mental/2694838890

Reflection # 17; Personal Photo, June 10, 2023

Reflection # 18; Photo Credit; Chris Zoeller, Waterloo Courier Staff Photographer, June 12, 2023

Reflection # 19; Spider Man, Site Credit – https://www.google.com/url?sa=i&url=https%3A%2F%2Fwww.

redbull.com%2Fgb-en%2Fspider-man-ps4-our-final-verdict&psig=AOvVaw2foN6eeigRlKfZpEc4ME-h4&ust=1719698044225000&source=images&cd=vfe&opi=89978449&ved=2ahUKEwjuztLJpP-GAxWftIkEHYycCVMQjRx6BAgAEBU

Reflection # 20; Lou Pinella, Site Credit – https://www.seattletimes.com/sports/game-of-the-day-sweet-lou-leaves-kicking-screaming/.

Reflection # 20A; Heart Image, Site Credit – https://br.ifunny.co/picture/good-the-heart-that-loves-is-always-healthy-the-heart-mSY7NOij9.

Reflection # 21; Vince Lombardi, Image, Site Credit–https://slideplayer.com/slide/4400083/

Reflection # 21A; Vince Lombardi, Article, Site Credit – https://www.capjournal.com/opinions/back-to-the-basics/article_bf1924a8-ab31-11ea-97a1-674813545028.html.

Reflection # 22 and # 22A; The Hill; Movie, Site Credit – https://www.catholicmom.com/articles/the-hill-a-movie-about-faith-and-baseball.

Reflection # 23, 23A and 23B; Matt Olson and Reece Blankenship, The Unspoken Bond Article; Site Credit – https://www.mlb.com/news/matt-olson-reece-blankenship-friendship

Reflection # 24; Pixabay royalty free image

Reflection # 24A; Personal Photo

Reflection # 25, 25A, 25B and 25C; Image with permission of Daryl Strawberry Site Credit: https://findingyourway.com/

Reflection # 26, 26A and 26B; The Daily Iowan; October 31, 2023, Site Credit: https://dailyiowan.com/2023/10/31/field-of-courage-liam-doxsees-life-with-scid/

Reflection # 27; Site credit – Free Image: https://unsplash. com/photos/person-holding-gray-heart-shape-ornament-4qHWTuP_RLw

Reflection # 27A; Pixabay royalty free image

Reflection # 28; The Love Foundation, Site Credit; https:// www.pinterest.com/pin/life-is-a-delight-when-we-share-our-love-and-light—249175791873349604/

Reflection # 29; Site Credit – shutteerstock.com–1944185056

Reflection # 29A; Roberto Clemente, Baseball Quotes; Baseball Quotes on X: "Roberto Clemente http://t.co/ Dt2quKXhBD" / X

Reflection # 29B; Pixabay royalty free image

Reflection # 30, 30B, 30C and 30D; Smithsonian on Jack Trice Site Credit: https://www.smithsonianmag.com/ history/this-black-football-player-was-fatally-injured-during-a-game-a-century-later-a-college-stadium-bears-his-name-180982989/

Reflection #30A; Buffalo Bills Kicker missing FG, Site Credit – https://nypost.com/2024/01/22/sports/ bills-tyler-bass-feels-terrible-after-wide-right-kick/.

Reflection # 31; Site Credit – Facebook; https://www.face-book.com/reflectionsfromthehometeam/

Reflection # 31A; Site Credit – Image with Permission of Atlanta Braves Inc.

Reflection # 31B; Personal Photo

Reflection # 32; Baseball Factory, Site Credit – https://www. facebook.com/photo.php?fbid=885679430029002&s et=a.520922989837983&type=3

Reflection # 32A; Don't Let the Old Man In, Site Credit – https://www.ebay.com/itm/296099289884

Reflection # 33; https://www.vector-stock.com/royalty-free-vector/cute-happy-baseball-cartoon-smiling-vector-21456338

Reflection # 33A; Photo courtesy of Atlanta Braves Inc.

Reflection # 34; Casey Stengel, Site Credit; https://i.ebayimg.com/images/g/14oAAMXQhpdRrRKd/s-l500.jpg

Reflection # 34A; Casey Stengel, Baseball's Greatest Character by Marty Appel, Site Credit; https://i.grassets.com/images/S/compressed.photo.goodreads.com/books/1478750586i/31377298.UY630_SR1200,630_.jpg

Reflection # 35; Personal photo

Reflection # 35A; Site Credit: https://thumbs.dreamstime.com/b/puppy-baseball-19982723.jpg

Reflection # 35B; Site Credit: https://thumbnails.cbsig.net/CBS_Production_Entertainment_VMS/2014/08/27/322565699982/ANDY_GRIFFITH_SHOW_THE_097_GOMERTHEHOUSEGUEST_1920X1080_1842244_1920x1080.jpg

Reflection # 35C; Site Credit: https://as1.ftcdn.net/v2/jpg/06/24/14/68/1000_F_624146827_JSdIv9JiukJ5Y6HAh3CvuD20wnwZaJns.jpg

Reflection # 36; Pinterest, Leo Buscaglia, Site Credit: https://i.pinimg.com/236x/8f/02/ff/8f02ff26a5e490e-6a258b443ae2be87b—good-funny-quotes-healing-hands.jpg

Reflection # 36A and 36B; Personal photos

Reflection # 37; Tin Man from Wizard of OZ – Site Credit: https://i.pinimg.com/originals/c0/55/9f/c0559f3a5e4fed-a9e5ae081f9da8eea7.jpg

Reflection # 37A; John Roedell, Picking up the pieces – Site Credit: https://barun.substack.com/p/im-falling-apart-can-you-put-me-back

Reflection # 38; Site Credit: https://img.ifunny.co/images/23c0d0949fa30fa3cae20622aebab58ad10af-34b4e012fdf7790fbd150d80375_1.jpg

Reflection # 38A; Never Give Up! Site Credit: https://i.pinimg.com/originals/53/2b/c5/532bc592c2b-031ec6978815da457e431.jpg

Reflection # 38B; Shine, Site Credit: https://i.pinimg.com/originals/ce/bb/c0/cebbc0bb0710c-798ba0d70b7dc94612e.jpg

Reflection # 39; Personal Photo

Reflection # 39A; Site Credit: https://i.ytimg.com/vi/iOW-UuhKzhk4/maxresdefault.jpg

Reflection # 39B: Personal Photo

Reflection # 40, 40A and 40B; Personal Photos

Reflection # 41; 2024 Olympic Gymnasts, Site Credit: https://i.pinimg.com/originals/f6/67/a7/f667a7ad-171fe86b4fa17b2352c40c85.jpg

Reflection # 41A; Site Credit: Pixabay royalty free image

Reflection # 42; Site Credit -https://media.istockphoto.com/id/618531888

Reflection # 42A; Site Credit–https://kcsattic.com/wp-content/uploads/2018/11/DSC07633-1017x1024.jpg

Reflection # 42B; What Happens Next? Book Image – Site Credit; https://www.amazon.com/What-Happens-Next-Travelers-Through/dp/1400260000

Reflection # 43; Site Credit: https://media.licdn.com/dms/image/C4D12AQFC7vUkKor8nA/article-cover_image-shrink_720_1280/0/16 11403698142?e=2147483647&v=beta&t=x mb-aFdyKX1p4othTMdxsi2H9Tc3hX76AC9IAlBYxlI

Reflection # 43A; Site Credit: https://i.ytimg.com/vi/qA1C-4MkWHuc/maxresdefault.jpg

Reflection # 44; Catherine DePasquale, Site Credit: https://quotefancy.com/media/wallpaper/3840x2160/7576146-Catherine-DePasquale-Quote-If-you-lived-my-life-you-wouldn-t.jpg

Reflection # 44A; Albert Einstein, Site Credit: https://cdn.quotesgram.com/small/66/51/798138726-2290376f045f-0c393a18245502f841ce.jpg

Reflection # 45; Dansby Swanson, Site Credit–Image with permission of Atlanta Braves Inc.

# *End Notes*

*Please note that all Scripture passages are taken from The New International Version (NIV) English translation of the Bible unless otherwise noted.*

1. *Extract from Thomas Jefferson to James Monroe, Paris, June 17, 1785*

2. *Pastor Brian King, Message at Nazareth Lutheran Church – July 17, 2022*

3. *Sparky Anderson, Excerpt from Steve Gilbert's Win Your Day – December 1, 2020*

4. *Jerry Salley, The Broken Ones – you tube https://www.youtube. com/watch?v=_KZP7j4cEOA&ab_channel=LloydAndrews*

5. *Warren Wiersbe, https://quotefancy.com/ warren-w-wiersbe-quotes/page/3*

6. *Dave Burchett, https://www.daveburchett.com/2015/04/07/ when-feeling-like-a-nobody-can-be-a-very-good-thing/*

7. *Dave Burchett, Site Credit: https://www.daveburchett. com/2022/09/19/the-games-people-still-play/*

8. *Samuel Johnson, Site Credit: https://libquotes.com/ samuel-johnson/quote/lbq5r7b*

9. *Charles Schultz, Peanuts, March 9, 1993–Site Credit https:// www.gocomics.com/peanuts/1993/03/09*

10. *Dave Berry, Article, Site Credit–https://www.elonnewsnetwork. com/article/2011/10/dave-barry-brings-the-laughs-coupled-with-sharp-insight October 11, 2011*

11. *John Mason, Author–https://www.amazon.com/Youre-Born-Original-Dont-Copy/dp/0884193551 June 1, 1993*

12. *Albert Camus, French Philosopher, Site Credit–https://x.com/ NYSPTA/status/1019205354029309952*

13. *Ann Lamott, Quotable quotes; https://www.goodreads.com/ quotes/9846-you-can-safely-assume-you-ve-created-god- in-your-own*

14. *George Springer and Mateo Sanchez, Article, https://www. mlb.com/news/george-springer-helped-writer-son-with-stutter March 2, 2023*

15. *Friend's Facebook Post, March 30, 2023- Site Credit; https:// www.facebook.com/limitless405church/photos/if-you-still- are-on-the-fence-about-about-going-to-church-this-weekend- for-easte/407973421991270/?paipv=0&eav=AfapFZ845 VBrS_MMmaaTrRzYNC1Uu1AxqswZszUjtdLbcCdq_a1s- qzU8SJXVa1EFI0&_rdr*

16. *Dave Burchett, Quote; When Bad Christians Happen to Good People; July 19, 2011*

17. *Hank Aaron, Quote; Site Credit–https://braveshistoryblog. wordpress.com/2018/10/24/my-motto-was-always-to-keep- swinging-whether-i-was-in-a-slump-or-feeling-badly-or- having-trouble-off-the-field-the-only-thing-to-do-was-keep- swinging-hank-aaron/*

18. *Dave Burchett, Is it possible to be optimistic in a pessimistic world? Article – June 10, 2024 – Site Credit; https://www.daveburchett.com/2024/06/10/ is-it-possible-to-be-optimistic-in-a-pessimistic-world/*

19. *Pat Jordan, A Nice Tuesday–https://www.amazon.com/Nice- Tuesday-Pat-Jordan/dp/0803276257–September 1, 2005*

20. *Byron Katie, Quote; Site Credit–https://www.goodreads. com/quotes/132449-when-you-argue-with-reality-you-lose- but-only-100*

21. *St Francis Assisi, Doing the Impossible Quote; Site Credit -https://catholicreview.org/doing-the-impossible/*

22. *Reece Blankenship, The Unspoken Bond, Article; Site Credit –https://www.mlb.com/news/ matt-olson-reece-blankenship-friendship*

23. *Glenn Hinson, We Need This Parable More Than Ever, Article; Site Credit – https://www.daveburchett.com/2022/07/18/ we-need-this-parable-more-than-ever/*

24. *Mary Matheson, Quote from the Daily Iowan, October 31, 2023; Site Credit: https://dailyiowan.com/2023/10/31/ field-of-courage-liam-doxsees-life-with-scid/*

25. *Mary Matheson, Quote from the Daily Iowan, October 31, 2023; Site Credit: https://dailyiowan.com/2023/10/31/ field-of-courage-liam-doxsees-life-with-scid/*

26. *Ben Wilmes, Quote from the Daily Iowan, October 31, 2023; Site Credit: https://dailyiowan.com/2023/10/31/ field-of-courage-liam-doxsees-life-with-scid/*

27. *Liam Doxsees, Quote from the Daily Iowan, October 31, 2023; Site Credit: https://dailyiowan.com/2023/10/31/ field-of-courage-liam-doxsees-life-with-scid/*

28. *Mercy Me, Lyrics to The Hurt and the Healer, Site Credit: https://www.google.com/url?sa=t&source=web&rct=j&opi= 89978449&url=https://www.youtube.com/watch%3Fv% 3DPmau3tkeEh0&ved=2ahUKEwiClcilsJWHAxVTpY4IHfrIC 4MQtwJ6BAg6EAI&usg=AOvVaw3lRobFGEvumSIfB256b5oH*

29. *Mother Teresa, Quote, Good Reads, Site Credit; https://www. goodreads.com/quotes/7969043-mother-teresa-s-anyway- poem-people-are-often-unreasonable-illogical-and*

30. *Jack Trice Quote, Smithsonian, Site Credit; https://www. smithsonianmag.com/history/this-black-football-player-was- fatally-injured-during-a-game-a-century-later-a-college- stadium-bears-his-name-180982989/*

31. *Mothering and Fathering your Parents, Personal note from a friend.*

32. *Devon Bandison, Let's Not Forget Why We Are Here–Site Credit; https://www.linkedin.com/pulse/ lets-forget-why-we-here-devon-bandison/*

33. *Clint Eastwood, Quote, Site Credit–https://www.billboard.com/ music/music-news/toby-keith-clint-eastwood-inspired-dont-let- the-old-man-in-the-mule-interview-8490429/*

34. *Toby Keith, Don't Let the Old Man In, Lyrics, Site Credit –* *https://killzoneblog.com/2024/03/dont-let-the-old-man-in.html*

35. *Mother Teresa, Let no one ever come to you without leaving better; Site Credit: https://www.goodreads.com/quotes/33359-let-no-one-ever-come-to-you-without-leaving-better*

36. *Casey Stengel,* Baseball's Greatest Character by Marty Appel, March 28, 2017

37. *Andy Griffith, The Andy Griffith Show, Site Credit: https://www.imdb.com/title/tt0053479/*

38. *Dave Burchett, Stay: Lessons My Dogs Taught Me About Life, Loss and Grace, Site Credit–https://duckduckgo.com/?q=The+passage+in+Dave+Burchett%E2%80%99s+book+Stay%3A+Lessons+My+Dogs+Taught+Me+about+Life%2C+Loss+and+Grace%2C+reads+as+follows%3A&iar=images&iax=images&ia=images&iai=https%3A%2F%2Fi.gr-assets.com%2Fimages%2FS%2Fcompressed.photo.goodreads.com%2Fbooks%2F1414602004i%2F22798885._UY630_SR1200%2C630_.jpg&pn=1*

39. *Leo Buscaglia, Speaker, University of Southern California – Site Credit: https://i.pinimg.com/236x/8f/02/ff/8f02ff26a5e490e6a258b443ae2be87b—good-funny-quotes-healing-hands.jpg*

40. *Wizard of Oz – Site Credit: https://www.threads.net/@keithgarnetmillar/post/C8nM48LqBxP*

41. *John Roedell, A Conversation with God – Site Credit: https://barun.substack.com/p/im-falling-apart-can-you-put-me-back*

42. *Phillip Yancey on Imperfection – Site Credit: https://www.daveburchett.com/2022/02/28/what-can-you-do-right-now-to-make-a-difference/*

43. *Billy Graham, Quote, Site Credit: https://www.brainyquote.com/quotes/billy_graham_626354*

44. *John O'Donohue, A Book of Celtic Wisdom, Site Credit: https://www.goodreads.com/work/quotes/72003-anam-cara-a-book-of-celtic-wisdom*

45. *Billy Graham, Site Credit: https://www.brainyquote.com/ quotes/billy_graham_626354*

46. *Max Lucado, What Happens Next?, Site Credit: https:// www.amazon.com/What-Happens-Next-Travelers-Through/ dp/1400260000*

47. *James "Gentleman Jim" Corbett–Site Credit: https://www. goodreads.com/quotes/540142-fight-one-more-round-when-your-feet-are-so-tired*

48. *Dave Burchett,* Stay: Lessons My Dogs Taught Me About Life, Loss and Grace Site Credit: *https://www.goodreads.com/book/ show/22798885-stay*

49. *Clint Hurdle, Daily Devotion, August 21, 2024: Site Credit: clint@clinthurdle.com*

50. *Albert Einstein, Site Credit:* https://cdn.quotesgram.com/ small/66/51/798138726-2290376f045f0c393a18245502f8 41ce.jpg

Milton Keynes UK
Ingram Content Group UK Ltd.
UKHW040401111224
452348UK00004B/340

9 798868 505102